Hope and Hard Truth

The publication of this book was supported by the
Lowell H. Lebermann Jr. Endowment for UT Press

Hope and Hard Truth

A LIFE IN TEXAS POLITICS

Mary Beth Rogers

University of Texas Press ⤜⤏ Austin

Requests for permission to reproduce material from this work should be sent to:
    Permissions
    University of Texas Press
    P.O. Box 7819
    Austin, TX 78713-7819
    utpress.utexas.edu/rp-form

♾ The paper used in this book meets the minimum requirements of ANSI/NISO
Z39.48-1992 (R1997) (Permanence of Paper).

Library of Congress Cataloging-in-Publication Data

Names: Rogers, Mary Beth, author.
Title: Hope and hard truth : a life in Texas politics / Mary Beth Rogers.
Description: First edition. | Austin : University of Texas Press, 2022. | Includes
bibliographical references and index.
Identifiers: LCCN 2021061600 (print) | LCCN 2021061601 (ebook)
    ISBN 978-1-4773-2573-5 (hardcover)
    ISBN 978-1-4773-2574-2 (PDF)
    ISBN 978-1-4773-2575-9 (ePub)
Subjects: LCSH: Rogers, Mary Beth. | Women politicians—Texas—Biography. | Texas—
Politics and government—1951–
Classification: LCC F391.4.R643 A3 2022 (print) | LCC F391.4.R643 (ebook) | DDC
976.4/063092 [B]—dc23/eng/20220126
LC record available at https://lccn.loc.gov/2021061600
LC ebook record available at https://lccn.loc.gov/2021061601

doi:10.7560/325735

For Lauren and Lindsey

Contents

Hope and Hard Truth

Into the Well

Truth is at the bottom of a well: look into it and you see the sun or the moon; but if you throw yourself in, there's no more sun or moon: just truth.
Leonardo Sciascia, Sicilian novelist and politician, 1921–1989

THE SURFACE OF A WELL'S cool waters might reflect glimmering images of the sun and moon, but the old well diggers in rural Texas and in the Sicilian hills of my ancestors always knew that rocks and grit and even snakes could be nestled in the darkness of the pit at the bottom. If the well became polluted over time, the grit would rise, the water would turn sour, and everything would change. I didn't know that fundamental fact as a young woman in the 1960s when I took my first dive into the deep well of Texas politics. But I learned.

Looking into the deep waters of a well seems to be the perfect metaphor for my old-age reflections on the wild and woolly world of Texas politics. That's because the deeper I looked, the more I learned about myself and the truths underlying the illusions and delusions I brought to the experiences that shaped my life.

My deep well of Texas politics was full of intrigue, suspense, tension, rage, risks, secrets, foolishness, and, yes, always a few snakes in its darkest recesses. But it was also full of joy, fascinating characters, exhilarating events, deep friendships, bold acts, and satisfying deeds. For a long time, I loved it all. But why on earth would a half-Sicilian girl who grew up in Dallas, Texas, be so hell-bent on diving into the muddy mix of politics? Why Texas? Why politics?

The clues were there from the get-go.

Like many people of my generation who grew up in Texas, I was captivated by the pastiche of Texas history and myth. It's a cliché to say that everything here is bigger—people and places, risks and rewards, self-created mythologies and glorious adventures. Most of us who were born here believed some form of the heroic myth. But the reality turned out to be quite different, particularly when confronting our total history. The extremes between rich and poor, the powerful and the powerless, were dramatic. The clashes of race, religion, gender, class, and culture always seemed apocalyptic, as if our very lives were at stake. And sometimes they were. But my magnetic fascination with the deep well of Texas politics drew me to causes and people who were rarely part of the accepted myths. So, whether it was destiny or pure foolishness, little by little, year by year, I plunged deeper into that well, only gradually coming to understand the complex realities beneath its surface attractions and glittering reflections.

I frequently saw things as I wanted them to be, sometimes even after the facts would seem to prove otherwise. I did not always grasp a fundamental truth that is often encapsulated in the old saying "The more things change, the more they stay the same." Sometimes what we assume to be a major change does not affect reality on a deeper level. That's why many of our authentic political struggles are never ending.

It was only after I moved from the center of the political world to its fringe that I could really come to terms with this fundamental truth and understand why I held on for years to all of my illusions and delusions about the kinds of politics I had come to love.

By dredging up some half-forgotten stories of the past, I also began to understand why I was so captivated by the hard-edged world of Texas politics, which has always had a wild rawness that allowed only the most ambitious, outrageous, wealthy, or ruthless players to thrive. But I was actually having such a good time in the midst of it all that it took a long time for that reality to sink in.

It is clear that my political impulses were developed within my parents' world, where their own experiences and heritage initially assigned them roles as society's underdogs. So I was naturally aligned with society's other underdogs—the poor, the powerless, the shunned, and the shamed. In the concept net that we all create, my quest centered on opening the doors for those of us who were traditionally shut out of politics and access to power. Of course, that meant that I was a liberal in a rigidly conservative state. To me, being liberal was more of an attitude toward life than a specific set of beliefs. It involved a "compassionate connection to other people," as *New Yorker* writer Adam Gopnik has written.[1] As such, the liberalism I espoused was not locked into some rigid ideology, historical antecedents, or dogma. It actually evolved and adapted to the changing conditions of the times. Fundamentally, it was a hatred of cruelty.

And Then Came Ann!

In the 1970s my political quest instinctively drew me to the emerging women's movement, which seemed to provide opportunities for women to prove that we mattered; that we too could play and win the game that determined the conditions of our lives.

Actually, we did win one—a big one at that. In 1990 we elected Ann Richards, the most scintillating politician of her time, to be governor of Texas. I got to run her campaigns and go along for the victory lap when I became her chief of staff. I actually loved the competition and all aspects of winning, even though it was never easy. Winning in Texas for those of us who were never part of the political or economic establishment has always been the ultimate—and rare—political experience. And I was lucky to have that experience. Winning allows you to know the secrets behind the headlines, and even as a gawky teenager I wanted to know those secrets. I devoured the daily news for hints. Why are things as they are? What caused this or that? Who made it happen? Why are some things so carefully hidden? What's really going on?

Although I had already been involved in local San Antonio politics for almost ten years before I really got to know Ann Richards, something fundamentally different was happening for me in the political world by 1971. Politically active women felt a new urgency to "do something more" in the world that had so long excluded us from opportunities for real leadership and access to authentic political power.

That urgency was manifest when Republican and Democratic women came together in 1971 to form the bipartisan National Women's Political Caucus. Congress passed the Equal Rights Amendment (ERA) to the US Constitution in 1972 and sent it to the states for ratification. The battle was joined.[2] Politics, destiny, and our own ordinary lives were changed when we plunged deeper into the muck to fight for ourselves, for expanded legal rights, and for an end to gender—and racial—discrimination. It was exhilarating. Yet for women of my generation—already in our thirties or older—our new political aspirations complicated our domestic lives with children, husbands, and work. And home life was still vitally important to us.

I had two babies before I was twenty-two years old—Billy and Eleanor were born a scant fourteen months apart. In the early years, my life was centered on my children and laundry, car pools, Eleanor's piano lessons and Billy's Little League baseball games. I always volunteered to be one of those elementary school "room" moms who brought cookies for holiday parties and Parent Teacher Association meetings. Later, as I became more involved in the world of work and politics, I became a master at finding good pick-up meals more often than I'd like to admit, because who had time to cook? I was always on the run because that's what we did. Women of my generation squeezed everything we could into the new opportunities that the larger world seemed to offer us, rushing off to one meeting after another and then hurrying home after work feeling guilty because we didn't have fresh-baked cookies waiting when the kids came home from school. Yet, I now realize, the choices I made during those years were more often expanded than limited because of my children.[3] From them I learned responsibility and the compelling power of love. They were always central to my journey with their father, John Rogers, through a marriage full of pleasures and pitfalls, like most long-term relationships. And we were fortunate that our family was able to make the most of this time together while we had it.

I think women of my generation were always torn when trying to balance home and family and all of the new opportunities that seemed to be unfolding in front of us in those early years. There was never enough time for all that we wanted or needed to do. I was continuously asking myself, "Should I be doing this or that?"—whatever this or that happened to be at the time. Perhaps that was one of the sources of the ambivalence that I frequently felt about so many of my experiences over the years. It played out in both personal and political ways, and for me the personal and the political were always mixed. As I look back on my life, it is hard to separate them.

It was initially disconcerting to recognize that I was alternatively active and passive, immersed and withdrawn, observant and oblivious, exhilarated and exhausted, dreamy and determined. For most of my time in politics, I often felt on the edge of the hustings, never quite totally inside but not quite all of the way outside either. That was because I was usually torn between an interior life of deep longing to "just be" and an exterior life of constant action. As a result, the outer events of my life were fairly sequential: one leading to another, flowing naturally and normally, while my inner life floated as an undercurrent, without continuity or sequence, yet emerging from time to time in some mysterious way.

Was there more than politics in my life?

Yes, of course. After my children were grown and settled into their own lives, I was lucky enough to write a few books and even become the chief executive officer of one of the best PBS stations in one of the most exciting cities in the nation: Austin, Texas.

KLRU-TV—now called Austin PBS—was the home of the longest-running music show in television—*Austin City Limits*. Our boosters were Nobel laureates and high-tech moguls, dopers and doctors, writers and artists, moms of toddlers and out-of-date hippies who dreamed of living off the grid. KLRU reflected progressive Austin's highest aspirations. I was fully committed to the values of public television and never experienced the kinds of conflict between words and deeds that my role in Texas politics often generated. I was proud of my work. But while I also had so many other opportunities—to teach, to write, to travel—it is still the political world that haunts me.

This much I have come to believe: when it's over no one else will know all that happens to us internally. The "phenomena in the mind" are private and not often open to inspection by others.[4] We simply store up experiences, unconsciously taking in events without exploring their meaning. Then, at some point, something pushes them out into our orbit of awareness, and we are often compelled to dive deeper into our inner world to come to terms with it all. What was illusion, and what was reality? And what really mattered?

The Continuous Thread

When I began the exploration of my metaphorical well, I hoped to find the threads that connected my inner and outer worlds as well as my public and private life. Finding those connections seemed to be the only way that I could finally dispense with both illusion and delusion and get to the truths at the bottom of that well. Because writing had always been my way to figure out what I thought and knew, I decided to organize my experiences into a series of topical reflections that contained some of the political and personal stories that most affected me. These stories in my narrative are not necessarily in chronological order, as in a more traditional memoir. They are simply the ones that have been pushed full force into my late-life orbit of awareness. Even though the events in our lives happen in a sequence of time, writer Eudora Welty believed that only when we look back are we able to find the patterns that reveal the true shape and purpose of our life. Maria Popova notes that it is from these patterns that we "wrest our personhood from our experience" through what Welty calls "the continuous thread of revelation."[5]

In my late-life orbit of awareness and in my explorations of the past that resulted in this book, I rediscovered a few of the threads that revealed some essential truths about my sense of "personhood." I looked for patterns. And, without the distractions of my youthful political obsessions, I began to find them. I realized that I had always seen the world through a political prism that was shaped by heritage, belief, and experience. That meant that I saw the world in terms of how society dealt with power and powerlessness, fairness and unfairness, privilege and poverty, economics and equality. Yet I was also always looking for something else that was deeper and more elusive—some sort of spiritual experience or knowledge that could explain it all. Maybe, as the Quaker writer Parker Palmer has suggested, a spiritual search can be an endless effort to penetrate illusion and touch reality. So that deeper search also turned out to be one of those threads of revelation that had guided my life.

Even more truths were revealed when I was able to dive deeper into my metaphorical well. The ambivalence that I initially found so disconcerting might not have been a sign of weakness, as I had feared. Perhaps it was an accurate response to events that I did not yet understand or to the possible outcomes that I could not predict.

The funny thing is, when I finally confronted the truths about politics that I found at the bottom of my well, I still held on to the conviction that the practice of authentic politics matters enormously in the overall scheme of things. It is essential to acquire the elements of life that provide hope and wholeness for a humane existence. It also requires a commitment to a never-ending struggle. Perhaps that was the ultimate hard truth among the many truths I discovered along the way. The most surprising feeling came with this hard truth: I still had hope, which is different from illusionary optimism. I learned that we can survive without full closure or final resolution as long as we can find contentment within some deeper level of existence, as I have fortunately been able to do at various times in my life. I think I just needed to make sense of what happened regardless of how it turned out.

How did I get to that clarity? That is the journey I have tried to convey in these stories and reflections that contain my "continuous thread of revelation." But I need to make a few disclaimers. My friend Ann Richards shows up in a lot of these stories because our political lives were so entwined for so long, but this is not her story. It is mine. And although tidbits of Texas history are woven into my stories, this is not a political history—only my view of some historical trends that shaped my life and the lives of other women of my generation who chose to be active in Texas politics.

Pete Hamill, the late great and gritty New York newspaper columnist whose opinions and books earned him a reputation as a tabloid poet, once tried to explain how we approach telling the stories and memories of our past. "Everybody's got three lives," he said. "A public life, a private life, and a secret life."[6] But maybe we have only one true story to tell, and our exploration has to blend them all. I have tried to capture my one true story—my truth—by weaving together the public, personal, and private threads.

For me, the public life was about politics almost all of the time. Most of my stories and reflections come directly from that public life and are familiar to many of my coworkers and friends. The private life was centered on family and love. My husband, John Rogers, and I shared a passion for politics, so our private time together was pivotal to understanding all that came before and after. But my secret life—the one I mostly hid from others—was lived within some deeper aspect of heart and soul and an inner force that I struggled to reconcile with everything else that dominated my time and energy.

When we dare to reveal our secret lives, it's ironic that our screwups—busted romantic relationships, bad decisions, and the kinds of stupid actions that are coated with guilt and regret—may not emerge front and center. I've come to believe that those are not the things that matter most as we age. Once dealt with through therapy, other kinds of internal audits, or external confessions, they are hardly interesting enough to be worth revisiting again, particularly if such revelations might bring distress to others. In my advancing age, it is those deeper and more soulful, secret interior yearnings that I most want to understand. They are the ones that lured me into the public and private ventures that shaped my vision and my life.

The paradox is that our deepest secrets often reside not in our deeds but inside ourselves—within our hopes and dreams that are ensconced within our own vulnerabilities. This vulnerability is most marked when we allow others to see how we really *want to be*, especially if what we want for ourselves is a better self. Revealing this deep urge can be particularly troubling if we have operated within the volatile and often cynical world of politics. We then allow others to judge our day-to-day behavior on the basis of our deepest idealism. Of course, being human, we usually fall short of true wisdom and open ourselves to charges of hypocrisy, naiveté, foolishness, or worse. We risk appearing as irrelevant to others in our late-in-life truth telling as the holy fools who show up in Russian novels. I know that I have been foolish at various times in my life. Perhaps adding the word "holy" to some of those actions might actually be a blessing.

Maybe the holy or foolish threads were there from the beginning. I just didn't know how to connect them. Now they can emerge in these stories from the well.

PART I
Winning and Losing

"Look, There's the Girl"

Was I dreaming? I was on a stage in front of a noisy crowd packed into an Austin hotel ballroom. I struggled to see the faces beyond the lights that were almost blinding me. I couldn't read the notes I held tightly in my shaking hands. But I had to do what I had to do and began by awkwardly introducing myself. The crowd erupted into cheers, whistles, and wild applause, less for me—I knew at the time—than for what I was about to say. So I just blurted it out, not even waiting for the noise to subside.

"Here she is. Your new governor of Texas!"

This was no dream. Ann Willis Richards, liberal Democrat, divorced mother of four, recovering alcoholic, and pro-choice feminist, had been elected governor of Texas that evening. It was one of those miracles of Texas politics that have emerged from time to time in our history. It was just that no one expected this particular woman at this particular time to carry off that miracle. But here she came, striding into the cheering crowd to the rousing chords of "Chariots of Fire." I had never seen such joyful chaos.

As her family joined her on the stage, I stepped back from the podium to give her the total space to enjoy her victory. But she pulled me back into her family huddle to stand with her as she had always done, starting with her first venture into electoral politics when she became a rather obscure local county commissioner. She wanted to make sure that I could share the accolades that would come her way.

In that moment, I was thrust into public life in a way that I had never imagined possible. So much had happened to get us to that moment. Only three years earlier, on that exact date in November, my world had been torn asunder. My husband, John Rogers, the real political operative in our 27-year marriage, had died suddenly. It was Ann Richards who had shown up on my doorstep to bring me an urn to hold his ashes.

So much before and after that moment harnessed my career to hers. And my life was forever changed.

IF I REALLY WANT TO look deeper into the well of Texas politics and its impact on my life, I have to write about the power of friendships that sometimes emerge from our political connections. My friendship with Ann Richards was one of the most unlikely of my life. My view of it is probably shaped as much by my fabric of illusions as by the hard doses of reality that were thrown into the mix.

Truth be told, Ann made everyone around her feel like a friend. Even little kids on school fieldtrips to the stately Texas Capitol building in Austin seemed to have an affinity with her. You could watch the faces of little girls light up when they gazed up at her official portrait in the magnificent Rotunda, surrounded by all those old white male governors of the past. Then you might see one of the girls shyly poke her buddy and say, "Look, there's the girl."

For a long time, I felt the same way about "the girl." She was marvelous to watch, but while others saw Ann perform with such panache on the political stage, I got to have a closer view from behind the curtain. While many were—and still are—drawn to that smart, strong, funny woman, there was so much more to her character than the quick quips that attracted her devoted fans over the years. She could be generous, kind, fiercely loyal, and amazingly thoughtful. Over the years, she somehow miraculously managed to mask her vulnerability while leading an intensely public life.

We became friends before she ever thought about running for office and remained so until her death from esophageal cancer in 2006. And because I was there early on, before so many others joined her remarkable ascent to the top of Texas politics on her way to becoming a national icon, ours was a reciprocal relationship—never a one-sided deal. When we worked together in various professional capacities, she was always solicitous of my privacy and my domestic life and never imposed on my snatches of free time when I needed to be away from her office or from one of the campaigns. Yet when we were faced with some sort of political crisis—and there were many along the way—she expected my attention and inspired my best efforts. She forced me to overcome my basic shyness and most of my fears.

Such a friendship took time to develop, and we had a good thirty-five years to figure it out, get used to each other, and find a balance that would suit two strong women who were so different in personality and style.

Ann Richards and I actually met at a much earlier time in our lives, and neither of us could have imagined that we would ultimately become friends on similar personal and political journeys. Ann lived in Dallas at the time with her husband and young children and had become friends with my mother when they were both active in a group called Study Action. Many of the members were younger women like Ann who had grown frustrated with respectable groups like the League of Women Voters because all they seemed to do was study issues: they rarely took action. So these women, and older women like my mother who had been involved with the League of Women Voters, started their own club that would both study a public problem and take action to solve it. John Rogers and I were living in San Antonio at the time. I was visiting my family in Dallas when my mother took me to a Study Action meeting, where I met Ann for the first time. I was heavily pregnant with my first child, and Ann was pregnant with her third child.

Our common condition was probably why we remembered each other almost ten years later when we were both living in Austin. Ann called me one day to invite John and me to one of her fabulous parties. "Your mama told me to call you and get you involved in Austin," she said. From that first call, and our common love of politics, we developed a friendship that evolved over the years. But our husbands were the activists in those early days in Austin; we were the bystanders and mothers of young children. David Richards was a noted civil rights and labor lawyer. John Rogers was a journalist turned political strategist who handled politics for the state labor federation. By the early 1970s, however, the new women's movement seemed to provide an opportunity for both Ann and me to participate more fully in the wider political world that we loved.

Our work together started when young Sarah Weddington, fresh off her victory as the attorney who successfully argued the *Roe v. Wade* abortion legalization case at the Supreme Court, decided to run for the state legislature. Ann, who had been a volunteer in dozens of campaigns, became her campaign manager. "Mary Beth, help me write this brochure," she would plead in her unique Texas twang. Or "Mary Beth, we need a mail piece to send to state employees. Figure out what to say and write it for us." And I did. We discovered that we could be an effective team, advancing progressive politics and women's issues.

As time went on, I became a kind of quiet alter ego to Ann's more flamboyant self, never out front unless she forced me to be, as she often did. I always stood a few paces behind Ann. She was the innovator. I was the implementer. I also became one of her challenges to "fix." She taught me how to cook fish and make vinaigrette dressing from scratch; she made me buy Ferragamo shoes and good clothes; and she turned over the functions of the State Treasury to me for long periods when I was deputy treasurer, her second in command. She pushed me to preside over meetings of the State Banking Board, testify before legislative committees, negotiate impossible deals, ask for money, manage unruly employees, and speak before crowds of a thousand or more. I did all those things and learned and benefited from them. Yet I was always a bit ambivalent about drawing too much attention to myself, but Ann kept pushing me to do more. And I did, at first somewhat reluctantly until I grudgingly adapted to my new role. Aside from my parents and my husband, few people had a greater influence on the outward course of my life than Ann Richards.

Ann touched me in so many ways that extended beyond politics or even ordinary friendship. And I was not alone in absorbing her influences. Her circles of friendship extended not only to women who were trying to make their mark in the world but to so many men she befriended, mentored, and opened doors for, thereby launching their own careers. She was adept at plucking young men out of obscurity, whether it was offering a young gay man a job working for her so he could escape his stifling homophobic, small-town upbringing or appointing Ron Kirk, a young African American lawyer, to be her high-profile secretary of state, thereby setting the stage that allowed him to be elected the first Black mayor of Dallas and still later to become President Barack Obama's cabinet-level trade representative.

Ann's relationships also extended to anyone who had the courage to show up at a meeting of Alcoholics Anonymous (AA). That included hundreds of men and women over the years who considered her a friend even if they never met her. Many of them left their AA sobriety recognition chips on the steps of the Texas Capitol building, where her body lay in state a few days after her death in 2006. Some of the chips were brand new, given out after the first thirty days of sobriety. Some were worn, representing ten years or more of attempting a life of "rigorous honesty," as she used to say. It took her a while to get to that point, she would admit, and some of the truths of her life did not come until near the end.

The Fear Factor

About a year before she died in September 2006, I had my last serious conversation with Ann Richards. We had talked off and on during her last year, but I knew this conversation was important to her. She told me that she had gained a profound insight. She realized that she had lived much of her political life in fear. Fear that she was not good enough or smart enough or tough enough or even funny enough to live up to her own reputation. She was afraid of mistakes and failures, of loss of love and energy, and mainly of being irrelevant. And because of this fear, she had lived as if each experience or accomplishment was temporary, soon to be lost. She even feared that, if she lost everything, she would end up as a bag lady living under a bridge. But after she left the governor's office, none of that happened. She had experienced her worst fears and survived. She was earning significant money for the first time in her life, because our mutual friend Jack Martin hired her to open the New York office of his Public Strategies firm, whose clients included Fortune 500 companies. Now, as she was entering her seventies, she told me that she had finally let go of the fears that had clouded her life. She felt no pressure to perform or play the role she had so successfully cultivated her entire life. Her life was full of friends and family she loved, and she could do anything—or nothing—if that's what she wanted in the moment. She felt freer and more peaceful than ever before.

Of course, I was not the only one she told when she had insights like this. She often shared them with other friends closer to her than I was, and we all felt important because she told us something so personal and obviously meaningful to her. Then we might hear the same revelation in one of her speeches months later, shaped into an aphorism, a tidbit of advice for an audience of adoring younger women. That's the way it was: the deep personal insight revealed something terribly important for her, but soon it would also become a part of her public persona, as if to warn others: "If I can live without fear, so can you—but you don't know it yet, and now that I've told you, deal with it!" That insight of vulnerability, so precious in her early discovery, would be hardened into a hammer to pound the rest of us. Sometimes we needed her hammer, as I did when I was younger and full of my own oscillating fears. But later many of us did not need it. If we stepped away to pursue our own destinies separate from hers, new celebrity friends would always be there to take our places in the entourage. But she would never fully let her old friends go, always returning for reassurance to those of us who knew her best, who understood her fragility, and who would still love and protect her until her death. We did so then and even afterward, as we mourned her too-early death from esophageal cancer and hastily threw together a lying-in-state ceremony and visitation at the Texas Capitol as well as a moving memorial service attended by thousands of admirers from all over the country.

Why did Ann have this hold on us?

Anyone who knew her learned how unique she was. She had a bullshit detector and could see the absurdity in most pompous people. But she could dish it out too, sometimes shocking even herself with her glibness and crowd-pleasing demeanor. She could be dogged, persistent, funny, daring, outrageous, ambitious, generous, wicked, brutally honest, caring, even careless and foolish in her early years, and brittle and bejeweled in her later life. Boredom was Ann's enemy. She was willing to try anything, especially if she could be the first in whatever she did.

In what she called her "good-old, bad-old days," she was probably the first hard-drinking woman to break into the equally hard-drinking old guard of the still powerful Texas Democratic political establishment. It was a source of pride for her to hang out at the old Quorum Club a block from the Texas Capitol building with Frank Erwin, confidant of Lyndon Baines Johnson and Governor John Connally. In his position as chair of the Board of Regents, Erwin almost single-handedly ruled the University of Texas, which was like a second seat of government in the state at the time. He was often described as the most powerful and vindictive man in Texas. But he laughed at her jokes, and she at his.

From her less than regal elected office as a county commissioner in the badges and beer belly domain of local government, Ann became one of the nation's first elected officials to speak out on pro-choice issues when rabid anti-abortion, right-wing reaction to *Roe v. Wade* began to sweep the country. She helped organize the first gatherings of elected women around the country in the mid-1970s. She encouraged and supported dozens of women who wanted to run for public office. More importantly, perhaps, Ann was one of the first politicians in the nation to go to "drunk school," the term she used to describe her 30-day treatment for alcoholism. When she returned from treatment, she stood alone in front of the incredulous Texas press corps to go public with her addiction. In the process, she became an inspiration to thousands of men and women all across the nation. In 1982, just a couple of years out of alcohol treatment, Ann won election as Texas state treasurer, the first woman to be elected to statewide office in Texas in over fifty years. Then she became the first woman elected in her own right as governor of Texas in 1990. Her wit, blunt honesty, and dynamic personality drew people to her. Perhaps it was the sparkling blue eyes or the shock of white hair or the strength of her gait. A Buddhist monk we met once in Santa Fe described her as a goddess. She was indeed one of those "sparklies" you rarely encounter in life, whose brightness is so blinding that you find yourself basking in the glow. A number of us in those early years were attracted to that blinding light and attached ourselves to its spreading beams.

Our Beginnings

During the 1970s, a half-dozen or so women like myself bonded with Ann in both political and personal causes. Jane Hickie was a smart young lawyer who more than any of us became Ann's confidante and closest friend. Our group included Cathy Bonner, a flamboyant business entrepreneur who could come up with an idea a minute. She created one of the first rape crisis centers in Texas as well as getting the state to fund a ten-year $100-million cancer research program. Others included Martha Smiley, a calm, thoughtful lawyer who later built one of the most influential law firms in Texas as well as a thriving cable television domain. Lawyer Claire Korioth, one of Ann's oldest and most treasured friends, became a steady and steadfast insurance reformer, who named her only daughter after Ann. Judith Guthrie, a young lawyer who won civil rights lawsuits for women in television, had been a lobbyist for a big law firm and knew her way around the Texas legislature. She later became a US magistrate. Ellen Temple had a passion for inclusion of women in Texas history and took the lead in publishing new works in the field. Katherine B. "Chula" Reynolds was a King Ranch heiress and philanthropist who expanded our influence into circles we could never have entered on our own. On the edge of the early political group was Suzanne Coleman, Ann's modest, indomitable speechwriter, who captured her voice in ways none of us could match. A dozen other women were close to Ann on a personal basis and helped her become the most popular officerholder in Texas, but this was the core group of political women who helped her from the beginning and with whom she always remained close. While Ann may have drawn our group together, we were also remarkably aligned in our common goals. We had a bias toward practical action and a belief that we could actually change our world.

We first came together to claim our history: women's history. It was Ann's idea, of course. She told the story again and again about how it all came about. She had taken her kids to San Antonio to visit the Institute of Texan Cultures, a marvelous celebration of the ethnic diversity of Texas. Ann's youngest daughter, Ellen, who was taking it all in, asked the question that launched our venture: "Where are all the women?" Where, indeed! So we decided to set out to find them.

Ann corralled me to organize and run a project to create a museum exhibit about Texas women—"Texas Women: A Celebration of History." It was an outgrowth of the larger Texas Women's History Project. Ann's group of friends, including lawyer Sarah Weddington, had created a nonprofit organization, the Foundation for Women's Resources, and set out to raise money for our project. We created an arrangement with executives at the Institute of Texan Cultures to stage an exhibition if we would do all of the work to put it together and pay for it.[1] Not realizing that we didn't know how to do it, we managed to bring it off—raising more money at the time than any women's project in the country had ever done before and putting together an ace team of staff and volunteers headed by the indefatigable Ruthe Winegarten.[2] Ruthe was an old friend of Ann's from Dallas who knew more about the new work on women's history than the rest of us. Her researchers were more like detectives than academic historians as they fanned out across Texas to search through museum warehouses, family attics, and local libraries. Sherry Smith, Frieda Werden, Melissa Hield, Mary Sanger, Janelle Scott, and others found hundreds of artifacts, photographs, letters, and journals of women who had written about their lives, whose accomplishments were usually hidden away in their husbands' papers in dusty historical archives. We even rediscovered lost facts of Texas's early suffrage movement and the names of women who had been elected to public office in the 1920s. Guided by historians such as Martha Cotera, we also discovered women of color who had been doubly ignored, perhaps honored in their own communities but unknown and disparaged in the wider culture of our raw state.

We organized our materials, identified patterns and themes, and conceptualized visually all that we had found. We began to tell compelling, even magical, stories about this underbelly of Texas history. I remember once when I had photos and old news clips spread across our dining room table, my skeptical then 16-year-old son asked me, "Are

Founding members of the Texas Foundation for Women's Resources, photographed in 2004: (back row, left to right) Katherine B. "Chula" Reynolds, Cathy Bonner, me, Martha Smiley, Ellen Temple, and Sarah Weddington; (front row) Jane Hickie, Judith Guthrie, Ann Richards.

you going to tell me that women did all those things?" And I could begin to tell those stories to him and to my daughter, as well as others, now backed up with photographs and artifacts.

We managed to open a blockbuster exhibit on Mother's Day in 1981 in San Antonio, headlined by Hollywood icon Ginger Rogers, and later took the exhibition to six major museums around the state over a two-year period.[3] It was a joyful exhibit that celebrated women in the context of the history and culture of Texas and was enormously popular with both women and men. Women's history in Texas ultimately became a cottage industry with new books and articles emerging, new leaders discovered, and women's studies programs created in Texas's most conservative colleges. Most importantly, our small group of women learned to ask for money and developed a network of progressive women and supportive men around the state.[4]

Under the direction of our nonprofit foundation president Cathy

Bonner and the supercharged dynamo Martha Farmer, who was a Presbyterian preacher's wife, we also created a nonpartisan leadership development program for Texas women. We invited women who were already active in their communities, nonprofit organizations, businesses, or professions to participate in a year-long program to explore Texas and its vast resources in the hope that they would ultimately become informed decision-makers who could hold positions of power and influence in our state. Over a thirty-year period, many of these women did just that, becoming mayors, members of the legislature, school board presidents, college administrators, and leaders in Texas's major corporations like AT&T, Southwest Airlines, Dell Computers, Texas Instruments, and others. Later we created a mentorship program called Power Pipeline to allow younger women at the beginnings of their careers to take advantage of the foundation's programs throughout the state.

Money, Money

As a result of these mostly nonpartisan efforts, we had connections with hundreds of women across the state and were armed with a newfound ability to raise money. Ann was able to build on this new base of informed women activists to launch a statewide campaign to become state treasurer of Texas. And lo and behold, she won! She asked me to become deputy treasurer, and for a time we were the two highest-ranking women in Texas government. We hobnobbed with bankers and bond lawyers and put together a professional staff headed by the young banker Paul Williams, who guided our efforts and knew the finer points about how to manage and invest Texas billions in tax revenue.

The Texas Treasury provided enormous opportunities for me to learn about the world of public financing, the money markets, and the banking industry. I had a big dictionary of key financial terms that I studied because, as Ann suggested, if we at least understood the lingo, we'd have a shot at understanding the intricacies involved in the investment of millions of dollars that flowed into the State Treasury every day. I learned how to write a prospectus for State of Texas bond issues and help organize the kinds of presentations we had to make to get favorable Wall Street ratings on the creditworthiness of the State of Texas. We made dozens of New York trips to market and sell Texas bonds. With Paul Williams at the helm, we managed to move the state's money management from quill pen and eyeshade days to a modern, automated operation. Because the state treasurer was a member of the board that issued state bank charters, and my statutory title of deputy treasurer gave me authority to cast votes and participate in decisions when Ann could not attend the regular meetings, I learned a whole lot about how money flowed in Texas through its state banking system. In the process, I was learning about much more than money. I was beginning to perceive the true nature of political power in Texas.

The Hairy-Legged Zoo Girls

Coming off our women's history project in the 1980s, we were riding the crest of the first achievements of the Second Wave Women's Movement in Texas. I guess we might have been a little too ballsy for some to take. After Ann Richards's election as state treasurer and as some of our successes began to mount, one of the old-timers in the state's all-white, all-male Texas political establishment had already dubbed Ann and her friends the "Hairy-Legged Zoo Girls."

Most feminists in the 1970s and 1980s who tried to enter the rough-and-tumble world of big-boy politics earned a derogatory sobriquet of one kind or another. And Hairy-Legged Zoo Girls was not meant as a compliment. Although many of Ann's core group of friends were simply opinionated housewives like me with children at home, a few newly minted lawyers, a few teachers, and several veterans from the nonprofit world rounded out the group. Almost all of us had volunteered in political campaigns and were serious political junkies. And yes, there were openly gay women in our group—a fact that raised hackles and horror in Texas politics at the time. It was fairly easy for troglodyte old guys to buy into a national negative stereotype of ferocious "bra-burning," men-hating feminists who wouldn't even shave their legs. The old politician who insulted us thought we simply belonged in a zoo with all of nature's other hairy creatures. Of course, we laughed this off, dismissing it as just one more negative comment from the old-guard politicians who resisted any kind of progressive change, particularly if women were involved. So we went on about our business, perhaps a bit delusional in our belief that insults like that really didn't matter, which of course they did. After all, we simply wanted to achieve enough power to make some changes in the antiquated state government of Texas.

And we did. A few years later, Ann decided to run for governor, against formidable odds. In the general election, I was enlisted to manage what looked like a quixotic effort at best. After a brutal Democratic primary in which Ann defeated former governor Mark White and Texas attorney general Jim Mattox, she started the fall campaign almost twenty-seven points behind her millionaire Republican opponent, rancher Clayton Williams. By sheer will in the difficult general election campaign that emerged, we managed to be organized, disciplined, focused, and even courageous. Ann became the perfect candidate. We had a cohesive effective staff and advisors and even had a plausible strategy largely shaped by Ann's long-time friend Jack Martin, who had a successful career in both politics and business. He became the campaign's most steady and significant advisor. Our inner circle included financial wizard Paul Williams and such stellar talents as former news reporters Glenn Smith, Bill Cryer, Monte Williams, and Margaret Justus. Young Matthew Dowd was our data-targeting guru. National consultants Harrison Hickman and Bob Squier handled our polling and media. When Ellen Malcolm and her new Emily's List national fundraising operation for pro-choice female candidates put money into Ann's campaign, we had a big boost and national credibility. But it was our own staff that did the heavy lifting, particularly Ann's son-in-law Kirk Adams and fundraisers Fred Ellis, Anne Wynne, and Jennifer Treat. All-around political operatives extraordinaire Richard Moya, Carl Richie, Billy Ramsey, Glen Maxey, George Shipley, Pat Cole, Nancy Kohler, Don Temples, and Joy Anderson, rounded out our core group with too many more to mention. Of course, every one of the Hairy-Legged Zoo Girls was deeply involved—Jane, Cathy, Martha, Ellen, Judith, Chula—the whole gang. Ann's four adult children—Cecile, Dan, Clark, and Ellen—were the secret weapons of the campaign, always willing to fill in wherever we needed them, traveling with their mother and making speeches and fundraising calls. Hundreds of volunteers worked daily in their local communities and took turns handling phones in our offices, managing the mail and our get-out-the-vote efforts.

With all of this excitement and help, we could seriously focus the dozens of activities and action steps necessary to carry out a strategy that was based on the numbers. We based everything on the numbers. We knew down to neighborhood precinct levels the numbers of votes we would need to have a victory. Our mantra became "If you can't count it, don't do it." That gave us a clear vision to determine exactly what needed to be done where, when, and how we might win a campaign that got off to such a rocky start.

We had to craft a narrative about who Ann Richards was and what she could do to create a "New Texas" based on what she had been able to do in the past. We had to find the best way to expose the emptiness of Republican Clayton Williams, who was a blowhard rich entrepreneur so far removed from the ordinary world of most Texans that he really didn't know what they needed or wanted. That was just the beginning. We needed to galvanize women voters who were eager to participate more fully in public life and see a woman win the state's highest office. We had to energize traditional Democratic voters to get out to vote, particularly Texas's large population of African Americans and Mexican Americans. Most importantly, to put Ann over the top on election day, we had to persuade undecided voters in the suburbs that she could deal with the issues they most cared about at the time: public education, insurance reform, and clean air. Part of that strategy was the promise to create a state lottery to help fund state government. One of our biggest challenges, however, was to raise the millions of dollars necessary to stay competitive in a race where we knew we would be outspent by a margin of at least two to one. That meant we

On January 15, 1991, Ann Richards was inaugurated as governor of Texas and spoke to a crowd of thousands gathered outside the massive State Capitol building in Austin. She sent this photo to me as her campaign manager and incoming chief of staff. (Photo courtesy of Alan Pogue)

had to manage our scarce resources carefully to be nimble and organized enough to create our own good luck by taking advantage of every opportunity that came our way. And we did.

Although we couldn't predict the outcome, we knew we were getting under the skin of our flamboyant opponent when he refused to shake Ann's hand in a widely publicized public forum on crime prevention, thus sealing his fate as a dolt and a brute who was an affront to traditional Texas chivalry. His sexist remarks about rape were so offensive to women everywhere that we began to see a few openings ahead. It wasn't until the final week of the campaign, however, that we were lucky enough to be able to launch a decisive strike that turned the tide. With data and numbers at hand, *Dallas News* reporter Wayne Slater got the Republican millionaire to admit that he had paid no income taxes in the previous two years. Because we had met our fundraising goals and had been careful in our expenditures, we had the funds to broadcast the shocking tax news all over our vast state.

When the votes came in on election night, it was clear that we had staged an upset victory such as Texas had never seen. Ann Richards, a liberal Democrat, recovering alcoholic, civil rights activist, divorced single mother, and pro-choice advocate, became a national icon for women and a hero for Democrats all over the country. We were euphoric. And I signed on to become chief of staff for the new Texas governor. But our euphoria was no match for the truth at the bottom of the muddy well of raw Texas politics.

We had our brief flirtation with power, and then we lost it.

A New Texas?

*Two days after Ann W. Richards was inaugurated as the forty-fifth gover-
nor of the state of Texas, President George Herbert Walker Bush sent American bombers to Iraq to push back Saddam Hussein's invasion of Kuwait.*

*More than 2,000 antiwar protesters, most of them students at the
University of Texas, marched from the campus to the Capitol building and
snake-danced around each floor of the massive Rotunda.*

*The chanting students pounded on the locked doors of the offices of the
people's governor. The Department of Public Safety, which was responsible
for the governor's security, brought in armed guards and locked us down to
prevent an "incident."*

It was certainly a hell of a way to begin the New Texas.

WE STARTED STRONG. ANN RICHARDS'S inauguration on January 15,
1991, was magic for me—and for 10,000 other Texans who marched up
Congress Avenue to the magnificent pink granite State Capitol building. Ann looked fabulous in her white suit, with friends and family
striding along with her. Ann's longtime family friend Virginia Whitten,
now in the final stages of terminal cancer, even made the trip in her
wheelchair. My parents were in the crowd, as were my children, Billy
and Eleanor, and my sisters and brother. The day was cold and crisp
but sunny and full of promise. There were a few glitches, of course, to
which we should have paid more attention.

Students at Texas Woman's University had designed and made the
beautiful white suit that Ann was wearing that day. But at the last
minute it had to be refitted. The governor's security detail insisted that
she had to wear a bulletproof vest under it, so the jacket had to be
enlarged and redone to accommodate the vest. That didn't dampen our

excitement. We didn't yet know that serious threats to Ann's safety were already coming her way.

I was eager to get started on Ann Richards's vision of the New Texas. I was fifty years old. After serving in various administrative positions in state and local governments, operating a small consulting firm, and running a few political campaigns over a ten-year period, I welcomed the opportunity to become chief of staff for the governor of Texas. After the parade, the inaugural ceremony on the steps of the Capitol, and a celebratory lunch in the stately Governor's Mansion, we explored our assigned offices in the Capitol building. I was thrilled to have the second-floor corner office with broad windows looking south toward Congress Avenue. It had been the office of one of the few progressive governors of Texas, Jimmy Allred, in the 1930s. Governor John Connally would later occupy the office for a brief period. But after the assassination of John F. Kennedy in Dallas, when Governor Connally was riding in the same car, the office of the Texas governor had been moved away from the windows and into a big windowless room deep in the inner-sanctum suite that Ann would now occupy. And it was a good thing, considering what had happened on our second full day in office. Still, we didn't let the student demonstration bother us. We had an ambitious agenda and wanted to get started. It was my job to manage it all and see that our work got done.

We brought in a talented staff of progressive experts who were knowledgeable in their respective fields: public education, insurance reform, air and water quality, utility regulation, health care, criminal justice, budget and tax issues. And we brought in a wonderful writer, Joe Holley, to create the written "blueprint" for the New Texas, so everyone could see what we wanted and intended to do. Because we had promised to open the doors of Texas government to those who had always been left out of policy decision-making that affected their lives, we immediately began appointing more women, Latinos, and African Americans to positions of power within various state agencies as well as the state's college and university systems. Ann's friend Jane Hickie initially kicked off the effort. Attorney Fred Ellis later took over the process to recruit and identify people of talent who could provide

Immediately after she won the election in 1990, Governor Ann Richards and key friends gathered at South Padre Island to plan the first 100 days of her new administration: Jack Martin and Ann Richards (kneeling in front), Cathy Bonner, Joy Anderson, Jane Hickie, Bill Cryer, me, Paul Williams, and Nancy Kohler.

leadership for the state's numerous administrative agencies. For the first time in history, a Texas governor began appointing openly gay men and women to major boards and commissions.

Under Ann's direction, her appointees began to take decisive action within their respective agencies. Beginning early in Ann's term, we were able to place a moratorium on new permits for commercial hazardous waste disposal until stronger environmental safeguards could be put into place. We initiated new air-quality rules for major industries. We diverted state and federal money into rural areas for water and sewage treatment services along the Texas-Mexico border, where some of the poorest people in America lived in third-world housing and health conditions. We took steps to clean up groundwater runoff into Texas streams and rivers from commercial development and agriculture pesticides. We placed consumer advocates on the state's utility and insurance commissions. We made it easier for disabled Texans to have home health care rather than be institutionalized in substandard facilities. We pushed for transparency in the awarding of major contracts within state government and imposed new regulations on substandard nursing homes. We even started alcohol and drug treatment programs for prison inmates to reduce recidivism.

Within progressive circles all over Texas, there was an outpouring of joy, hope, and pride, evidenced by the amazing volume of mail that the governor's office began receiving. An average of more than 7,000 letters a month flooded our office, which was more than the previous governor had received in an entire year. We created an Ombudsman's Office to help many of those letter writers, who believed that Ann could—and would—help them solve their various problems within the state's massive bureaucracy.

Still, with these flurries of appointments and policy initiatives that the governor could deal with through executive actions within many state agencies, we still had to deal with the volatility of the Texas legislature, which had begun its five-month biennial session a week before Ann's inauguration. We hired centrist Democratic legislator Jim Parker to handle our dealings with the legislature. While I had been on the fringe of legislative activities at various times in my career, I had never had direct day-to-day involvement with the process or the key operatives who had the power to run things. Jim Parker became my teacher. He was a big, lumbering guy with street smarts and great intellectual gifts. As a criminal defense lawyer in rural Texas, he used to carry his legal papers in a paper bag and spill them out on the defense table when he went to trial. His country-boy routine usually worked with a jury and turned out to be an asset in the legislature too. Because of Jim's work and Ann's willingness to dig into the details to cultivate key legislators, we had an amazingly productive first session.

Perhaps the most significant accomplishment of that first legislative session was the passage of legislation to force insurance regulators to protect consumers rather than only big insurance companies. The goal was to set a ceiling on rate increases that could be charged in any given year, and we had to hammer out key elements in the current law by constantly pushing and ultimately forcing compromises between

Governor Richards (left) with legislative director Jim Parker (standing) and me (right), working through a weekend in the governor's office to review bills passed by the state legislature during Richards's first year in office.

consumers and the key industry players. It was one of those rare feats where all the players got something they wanted—but not all that they wanted.

While Jim Parker and our team did the heavy lifting on our legislative program, including getting new ethics and financial disclosure requirements for state officials, I was constantly working with our young staff to keep our focus on our key issues, rather than all the "blue sky" ventures that warmed our liberal hearts. It was always a struggle to distinguish between all the things we wanted to do and the things that we might be able to do. We basically had two separate audiences that would measure our performance—an inside audience and an outside audience. We had to understand the difference between them and the need to please both of them in very different ways. The insiders our staff most wanted to please were the Austin liberals, the policy advocates, and other single-issue idealists who cared passionately about their causes and never wanted to see any kind of compromise. But our outside audience was made up of the vast majority of voters who had supported Ann and were more conservative than we were. It was critically important that we could deliver what we had promised them, including insurance and ethics reforms and the creation of a state lottery that would bring in much-needed new revenue to the state.

During those first few months in office, with the volatile legislative session occupying most of our time and attention, I was running on pure adrenaline. Our days started early and lasted well into the evening. To my surprise—and horror—I loved it. I felt alive and fully engaged in worthy struggles. It was not necessarily a happy feeling. I did experience some trepidation about the impact of the long hours and constant tension on both my physical and mental health. I often feared that I might become one of those action junkies unable to be still long enough to reflect on deeper ideas or long-term strategies. Yet it was not all drudgery. Sometimes it was just plain odd.

Early in Ann's administration, the president of Mexico came calling. Carlos Salinas de Gortari was in the United States to meet with President Bill Clinton and build support for the proposed North American Free Trade Agreement (NAFTA). Meeting the governor of Texas was his first stop. Salinas was the first of a number of foreign dignitaries who would visit Austin during Ann's term, so we carefully studied protocol and appropriate behavior when greeting a foreign head of state. About an hour before Salinas was to arrive at the State Capitol, however, we noticed that the Mexican flag in the governor's formal reception area had been affixed to its brass standard upside down and held in place with an unsightly bunch of Scotch tape. To avoid an insult to the Mexican president, as well as an international incident, we hurried to dismantle the disastrous flag placement. Someone in our office found a needle and thread. Ann took over, got down on the floor, and stitched the flag correctly to ropes on the brass fixture in accordance with proper flag protocol. Then she took her sewing needle into the governor's reception area where the news media had already gathered and proudly told the reporters what she had done. When Salinas showed up a few minutes later, a buoyant Ann made the most of this perfunctory visit.

During all that was going on both ceremonially and substantively in those first few months, we managed to keep our focus on what was most important to the voters and to ourselves. That allowed Ann's own amazing instincts to come into play. Our staff was able to provide the information and support that allowed her to act with unbridled confidence and charm. However, some major issues—like the state's biennial budget and appropriations bill—had not yet been resolved when the legislative session came to its mandated close, so we knew we had to prepare for a special legislative session over the summer. Ann and our senior staff retreated to a quiet spot away from the Capitol to plan our next few steps—just as we had done before she took office.

Pride Goeth before a Fall

Our planning for the upcoming legislative session got a bit out of hand. We were probably a little too proud of ourselves because of our successes during the first few months in office. In a brash moment of hubris, we decided to take on a total reorganization of state government by streamlining and consolidating hundreds of regulatory and oversight functions then spread across multiple agencies. That meant we had to come up with a plan to build support for our mammoth undertaking. On top of that, we also wanted to reform loose management practices in the awarding of millions of dollars of state contracts to private companies. It seemed like pretty dull stuff to outsiders, but it could be a big, troubling deal to insiders in state government. At the time, I wondered if we were carrying enough momentum from the regular session to be successful in these new ventures, because we still had to focus on budget and tax issues in the upcoming session. But we figured that a meaningful budget could be linked to a more efficiently run state government. It all seemed to be of a piece. Ann was enormously popular. Why not push for more?

What I don't think we realized at the time was that our successes initially moved along at such a rapid pace that they created shock waves among Austin's high-dollar lobbyists and their powerful Texas clients. Some of our most important actions were direct assaults on the oil and chemical industry, the major electric utilities, the mammoth insurance industry, and the bankers and lawyers who served them.

As it turned out, our appointees to a lot of boards and commissions were also upsetting their most important clients. Over the years, many of Texas's major industries had enjoyed minimal interference in their actions because most state regulatory agencies provided such lax oversight that it was almost nonexistent. Lobbyists for the chemical industry were appalled that we put environmental activists in positions to better oversee—and stop—recurring release of toxic fumes into the air or dangerous waste into rivers and streams. Insurance industry moguls didn't want consumer advocates messing in their business when they habitually refused legitimate damage claims from property owners or arbitrarily raised rates. The privately owned utility companies didn't want regulation of their transmission lines or rate-setting apparatus. Finally, big-time lobbyists didn't quite know how to deal with all those women and Black and Brown people who now had authority over some of their actions. They were not happy, and many lobbyists I knew personally or had worked with over the years on various projects were not shy about letting me know it. Some of them finally figured out that it might be a little easier to deal with the diversity of regulators—not to mention the staff in the governor's office—if they hired a few more women and people of color when they had to present their cases to these new bosses. A little-noticed, unintended consequence at the time was that many of these firms undertook mini–affirmative action programs within their organizations to bring in more women and minorities. Although some of them tried valiantly to adjust to the diversity aspect of the New Texas, it was a bitter pill for many others to swallow.

We had obviously stirred up a hornets' nest. This was hardly a surprise to political insiders, but we were often oblivious to the rawness of pure economic power. We never fully anticipated the harshness of the retaliation we might face with our plans for the massive changes necessary to bring about a New Texas. We also never anticipated the powerful statewide organizational structure that Karl Rove and the Republicans were putting together with money and moxie as they capitalized on the furor we were creating with our desire for change.

Paying the Price

We were probably a bit delusional in our belief that our actions were so popular with the general public that we would ultimately prevail. And Ann Richards was amazingly popular. Yet, as the months in office wore on and the opposition hardened in both the Texas House and Senate, it often felt like we were simply stuck in the muck at the bottom of our idealized well of Texas politics. Because the most powerful lobbyists had deep ties to key leaders in the Texas legislature, it was becoming harder to implement even small incremental changes. We would think we had achieved a compromise on some key piece of legislation only to find that our agreed-to-provision had "accidentally" been left out in the technical review by the time the bill came to the floor of the state Senate for a vote.

Once we thought we had agreement with both Texas Senate and House leaders on one of our regulatory reform bills that would consolidate several duplicate regulatory functions scattered throughout state agencies. But, after weeks of delay, we couldn't seem to move the bill out of one of the House committees. I took the bill home one night and read it slowly, line by line. It finally dawned on me that one powerful interest group would be adversely affected by the consolidation of regulatory powers: the *liquor industry*. The regulation of various aspects of the industry was shared by several state agencies that rarely attracted public attention. A stronger, consolidated, and more public rule-making authority could affect the liquor industry in multiple ways. And the major distributors, marketers, and sellers of beer, wine, and liquor were represented in Austin by a couple of congenial lobbyists known affectionately as the Booze Brothers.

The Booze Brothers were enormously popular with many legislators

because they often got free wine and beer donated for legislative receptions and parties. Their political contributions flowed freely to both
Republican and Democratic campaigns. As a result, they had a lot of
friends in the legislature, including the Speaker of the House, who had
assured Governor Richards that he supported the new regulatory bill.
It soon became clear, however, that the Speaker and his friends were
never going to let the bill come out of the committee. It would die an
ignominious death without much notice or care. The joke was on us.

I don't know why I was so surprised when I realized what was holding up the legislation. I guess I was delusional enough to believe that
if you had a deal, you had a deal. But that was not always the case.
Insiders in the game always understood: even if you *thought* you had a
deal, you had to be constantly vigilant to make sure it would hold. If I
had known earlier, we probably could have made a deal with the Booze
Brothers to mitigate some of the industry's concerns in order to salvage
the overall legislation. But then again, it was probably easier for them
just to kill the regulatory bill than to have to deal with "those women"
in the governor's office. Live and learn.

Episodes like this, plus the constant intrigue and multiple obstacles in our path, fueled my growing frustration. Under constant attack
by the naysayers and the state's official Republican Party apparatus, I
could see that our staff was running out of steam as we entered Ann's
second year in office. I was not sure that we were always on the same
page or speaking with "one voice" to avoid confusion or disarray. I could
tell that Ann was also a bit weary. She was on the go constantly. Sometimes the fame and glory of national events were a lot more fun than
slogging away in the daily grind of the Texas legislature. Ann was a star
in national Democratic Party circles, a much sought-after speaker and
campaigner for others. She was on call to help women who were running for office all over the country, and it was hard for her to say no.

In many ways, Ann's national prominence was often an asset to all
that we were trying to do in Texas. Many officials in state government
and in local governments across Texas were simply in awe of Ann. They
wanted to win her approval and enact her policies. They showered her
with praise and sought her favors. But there were others, particularly at

high levels in Texas government, who were jealous of both her national fame and local popularity. It was also becoming obvious that a small cabal of legislators simply delighted in sticking it to "that woman" in the governor's office, no matter what she proposed. The official Republican Party apparatus was launching regular attack missiles targeting some of our more ambitious goals, so we were also beginning to face more intense press scrutiny. I don't think we realized that incipient chaos would always be involved in governing at the highest levels and that the intensity of criticism would always be proportional to the impact of the changes we proposed.

The daily grind and annoying rhythm of attack and response began to take a toll, particularly when it was aimed at specific staff members who—some critics claimed—were guilty of zealous overreach. Our young staffers were easier targets than the ever-popular Ann Richards. However, it didn't take too long before Ann herself came under attack for pushing the boundaries of her executive leadership. Something had shifted with the Capitol crowd and perhaps internally in our office as well. It was time for a bit of self-examination, with the understanding that we were going to have to be more disciplined, focused, and much more practical to have continuing successes.

As we bumped along trying to regain our momentum, I realized that Ann was the one who ultimately suffered from the intensity of disapproval and critical judgment when our actions or inactions generated controversy—not the staff. Because of our long-standing friendship and my official position as chief of staff, it was my job to help her find her own balance to pursue whatever gave her satisfaction or to avoid whatever created consternation for her. Although she depended upon me to advise her about what I thought we should or should not be doing, I learned to temper my advice to allow her time to develop her own best course of action. That meant I had to avoid being distracted by petty feuds or useless brawls and concentrate on what really mattered—both inside and outside of the governor's office.

A wise friend used a religious metaphor to help me regain my own focus within the turmoil and stress of the daily grind. She suggested that I pose this question to myself: "What am I 'called upon' to do?"

Where could I make the greatest contribution within the daily chaos of governing? The question helped to focus on what was absolutely essential, rather than merely extraneous or immediate. It helped me pull away from micromanaging every tiny staff detail on every single issue out of fear that someone might make some mindless mistake that could halt our progress. I had to figure out how to make the best use of my time and energy to act decisively whenever a real crisis popped up. And, of course, there would always be a crisis of some sort that would require focused, strategic attention. When I began to look at my daily life this way, it was far less overwhelming but certainly not much easier. Still, a deep fatigue resulting from the long hours and fast pace was settling in as a "new normal" for me, with numerous petty confrontations that I could not avoid.

One day a state senator actually jumped up and down in my office, demanding that Ann attend a function in his district. Another state senator angrily blamed me personally and vowed revenge when Ann didn't appoint his favorite candidate to a vacant judicial post in his district. Some legislators and lobbyists believed that I always had the final word with Ann—much more power than I actually had as her chief of staff. I could be a villain or a hero on any given day depending on whether or not they got what they wanted from the governor's office. But that was my job. Most of the time, I could accept this reality as the cost of doing business in a volatile environment. But sometimes it could be downright strange.

One devilish issue brought us into conflict with a high-level public official, who was furious with Ann because he believed she had shown him "disrespect." When the time came to work out a deal to solve the problem, he refused to talk with Ann. He flat out told her that he would only talk to me, as if insulting her would be a satisfactory measure of revenge for him. Perhaps he even wanted to drive a wedge between Ann and me. It didn't work. Truth was that Ann didn't care one bit about stuff like that, and she laughed it off. It all seemed so juvenile—but that was the Texas legislature, of course, where ridiculous antics have always been part of the mix.

After we had fought our battles through two legislative sessions and a dozen state agencies and were almost at the end of Ann's second year in office, my fatigue finally caught up with me. The daily grind was wearing me down. It began to show up, sometimes in ways that at least gave us a good laugh.

Early one morning I was presiding over our regular staff meeting when someone started shrieking with uncontrollable laughter, pointing at my feet. As I looked down, I could see what brought on the gleeful braying, now coming from everyone in the room. I had on one black shoe and one brown shoe, and the heels were even of different heights! I simply had not noticed.

The staff was obviously delighted that my usual calm, disciplined demeanor at those meetings could dissolve in a moment of careless early-morning grooming. Of course, I had to laugh at myself too. But the moment gave me pause. If I could be oblivious to my own shoe color and style, what else was I missing? As time went on, I was also becoming increasingly uncomfortable with my own expanding public role in the governor's office, never quite as behind-the-scenes as I would have liked. Maybe it was time to move away from the public glare and constant turmoil of my high-profile position. Maybe it was time to stop long enough to organize my shoe closet. And an old friend gave me the opportunity to do just that.

Former state senator Max Sherman from Amarillo was now the dean of the Lyndon B. Johnson School of Public Affairs at the University of Texas. He thought I might provide some valuable information to offer his graduate students who wanted to enter public service or at least understand policy making in government. When he offered me the opportunity to teach there, I jumped at the chance.

Ann was not surprised when I told her I was leaving. "I've been waiting for the other shoe to drop," she quipped. Ann knew I did not like to be the public face for our ventures, But she also knew the inclination of my bleeding heart. She told a mutual friend, "I guess I'd have to open a soup kitchen in the governor's office to get Mary Beth to stay."

It was a great line, of course, and I had a good laugh when I heard it. I have to admit that there was always a bit of tension between my practical self and my liberal impulses. It was becoming clear to me, however, that I no longer wanted to be the daily crisis manager in the governor's office.

I believed that the opportunity to take a break would give me the time to think more clearly about the simple question posed by my friend about what I was really "called upon" to do. So I left the governor's office, but not Ann. As many of us in the political world learn, you never quite move out of the orbit of a charismatic and principled leader you admire and love. I willingly, and loyally, remained at Ann's beck and call for the rest of her term and beyond.[1]

Respite, Renewal, and Return

Teaching was a godsend for me. I loved my students and was inspired by their idealism and brilliance. Many have remained friends as they moved into careers in politics, business, or government. In order to be a worthy teacher for them, I had to read, think, and organize my thoughts and experiences in ways that began to make sense in overall schemes of power and process. I found wise words in great thinkers and profound political actors that seemed to express what I felt and believed but never fully grasped. I could finally begin to articulate in a more coherent way what the Czech dissident turned democratic leader Vaclav Havel had called the "rule of everydayness." It simply meant that experts, politicians, and policy makers need to understand what ordinary people do every day of their lives, what they struggle with, what is hard for them, what they really need, and what would make life's difficulties more manageable, if not easier. More importantly, what are their fears and hopes? The great American policies that actually worked followed this unarticulated rule of everydayness, as do Social Security, Medicare, public education, food stamps, and numerous regulations that provide for clean air and water plus general safety in almost all aspects of life. Although I didn't yet have a name for the rule of everydayness, I had actually experienced its impact much earlier when my husband was ill and we spent four years off and on at M. D. Anderson Cancer Center in Houston. Yet, when so few political players actually live in the ordinary world of ordinary people, it can be a challenge to discover the rule of everydayness.

While I was safely ensconced in academia, pondering ideas that fascinated me, I was still tangentially connected to the day-to-day political world of Ann Richards. I felt helpless as I watched what happened next.

The public attacks on Ann's administration, staff, and policies intensified soon after I left. I hadn't seen the looming disaster on the horizon. By late 1993, however, we knew that George W. Bush was in the wings, ready to hit Ann hard with a slash-and-burn strategy that could make him governor. In the 1994 reelection campaign, Ann would have to face a better organizational effort and a more appealing challenger than Clayton Williams had been in 1990.

A few of us who were close to Ann both personally and politically decided that we wanted to let her know of our concerns and perhaps spare her—and ourselves—from the defeat that we knew might occur. So Jack Martin and I, plus a few others trusted by Ann, sat down with her one day over lunch and tried to paint an alternative and appealing picture to show Ann the kind of role she might have in national politics if she decided to forego reelection and simply campaign for any number of potential Democratic successors who were waiting in the wings. She did not have to be the governor of Texas to be a national leader for the advancement of women or the progressive causes she cared so much about. She could lead from outside of the fray.

Ann would have none of it. She felt an obligation to all of her friends and followers who had sacrificed so much to help her ascend to the governor's office and believed she would be letting them down if she did not run for reelection. So the race was on, and I was enlisted to chair her reelection campaign. I had the hubris to think that I might be able to turn around what already looked like a problematic effort, just as we had been able to do in 1990.

I was wrong.

Reality

Reality is having my phone ring at 2 A.M. on three consecutive nights during the heat of the campaign and understanding that these hang-up calls are simply dirty tricks designed to unsettle me and increase my growing paranoia.

Reality is having a security firm routinely sweep the campaign offices for "bugs" because I fear that there are listening devices everywhere.

Reality is having our pollster tell me that he's seen a drop in the overnight tracking numbers, but it is nothing to worry about because it will "all even out." I fear the worst and believe that he's probably just trying to make me feel better.

Reality is learning that one of our campaign staffers got into a public shouting match with a famous college football coach in the lobby of a swank Dallas hotel, and I dread reading how it will play in the headlines the next morning.

Reality is finally realizing that I was not at the top of my game and never totally in control.

The ultimate reality, however, is accepting the Buddhist notion of impermanence. Life is always in motion. We arise, change, and decline. Nothing lasts forever—especially in politics.

ADAM GOPNIK, THE *NEW YORKER* writer, argues that one of the things that principled conservatives hate about liberals is that "liberalism, with its emphasis on reform, is an instrument of rapid change."[1] Rapid change is often a destabilizing experience for those who fear change of any kind, particularly when it involves a loss of power. In the governor's office we had been rushing headlong into the kinds of rapid change that would drastically alter the balance of power in Texas, which of course was going to raise the ire of those whose power and dominance would be affected. However, "principled" conservatism had little to do with the organized opposition we faced in the 1994 election. I came to believe that it was simply the fear of losing control of the apparatus of government that granted favor to a few at the expense of the many.

George W. Bush was to be the vehicle that would allow the powerful interests that Ann Richards had so alienated to return to what they assumed to be their rightful place in charge of the institutions of Texas state government. But George Bush was no Clayton Williams, who had proven to be little more than a wealthy, inept windbag in the race against Ann in 1990. Bush was charming, pleasant, and disciplined enough to avoid the offensive comments that had turned off women and suburban voters in the earlier race. He was never personally insulting to Ann, even after she threw a few biting barbs at him. Besides, he had the name and the political and business connections of his father, former president George H. W. Bush, who was deeply embedded in the nation's oil and gas industries through his earlier Houston ties with the giant Pennzoil Oil company.

The seeds of Ann's defeat had actually been sowed from the very beginning of her term, which was one of the reasons that Republican Party attacks began so early in her administration. Republican Karl Rove had correctly figured out that Ann's 1990 victory was a last-gasp Democratic blip in a growing Republican tide. Texas demographics were rapidly changing with the growth of the upper-middle-class Republican-leaning suburbs around Dallas, Houston, and Austin. The advances of the civil rights movement had begun to erode the white Democratic base vote in rural areas. If Rove could highlight the cultural issues that would inflame older white Democrats and provide an acceptable Republican alternative that could lure the new suburbanites away from Ann, then he would find a way to make George W. Bush governor of Texas. He found lots of ways. But no matter what the glossy TV ads said or how gracious Bush turned out to be, the cultural issues remained a core element that would be used to mount a winning campaign against Ann Richards.

As the old saying goes, "No good deed goes unpunished." Every good

Deputy chief Paul Williams (left), me, and budget director Dale Cramer (right), preparing to testify at a legislative hearing about the governor's budget proposals.

deed we felt we had been doing in the governor's office brought down the fires of hell during the campaign. Some of the acts we were most proud of became the source of almost daily attacks from a revitalized and hyperorganized Republican Party. Our environmental policies were characterized as "private property takings." Our effort to put more money into rural and poorly funded local school districts was labeled as an attack on wealthy suburban school districts. Placing more women and people of color into high-level positions, both within the governor's policy staff and as heads of state agencies, was seen as a threat to the all-white, all-powerful establishment that had controlled Texas since its beginning. Stopping toxic runoff from agricultural pesticides was viewed as "antifarmer." Providing drug and alcohol treatment programs for prisoners was characterized as coddling criminals.

Even more effective were the bizarre attacks on Ann claiming that she had lied about how lottery income would be spent as the proceeds began coming into the state's coffers. The new money had been designed to go into the state's general revenue fund all along to avoid a tax increase. The Bush campaign claimed that Ann had promised to use the lottery money exclusively for public education. Although that had never been part of her campaign promises, or the lottery bills passed by the legislature, the charge had sticking power and further weakened campaign efforts.

But the coup de grâce came when Ann vetoed a bill—at the urging of law-enforcement organizations—that would have allowed Texans to carry concealed handguns. The die was cast.

By early fall, when the contest entered its most serious phase, two campaigns were underway against Ann: the underground campaign focused on cultural issues and the more visible television campaign that featured an attractive and respectable George W. Bush, who could be trusted to bring law and order to Texas. For a variety of reasons, we were not particularly successful in countering either of them. We were not as nimble as we had been during the campaign in 1990. We couldn't settle on an issue that attracted many of the moderate suburban voters we had won in the earlier campaign. Because of infighting and suspicion among some statewide Democratic officials, we didn't have a unified get-out-the-vote strategy that was as effective as our efforts had been in 1990. We also were probably overstaffed, with a bifurcated campaign structure that couldn't always quickly counter the myriad charges leveled against Ann before they got lodged in the fog of public consciousness. Those charges came fast and furiously and in multiple forms and formats.

Ann was going to take away people's guns.

She was going to confiscate private lands without the owners' permission for her nefarious purposes (like pollution controls).

She had surrounded herself with "homosexuals" who pushed an agenda that was going to destroy families.

She was going to destroy the schools by robbing the rich school districts and giving the money to the poor ones.

Of course, these charges, as well as others just as inflammatory, came in so many different forms that it was hard to keep track of them, much less counter them. And we were having a difficult time shifting the dialogue to other issues more critical for the future of Texas.

There was even a baseless charge that resembled the infamous "Willie Horton" prison release ad against Democrat Michael Dukakis in the 1988 presidential campaign of the elder Bush.[2] It had worked to help elect George Herbert Walker Bush to the presidency, so we should not have been particularly surprised that the same fearmongering tactic would be used in the younger Bush's gubernatorial campaign.

During the final weeks of the campaign, Bush's staff floated a story that Ann had gotten an early release from prison for an old friend, who promptly murdered two elderly people during the course of a robbery. He was quickly caught, convicted, and thrown back in prison. When he was arrested for the murders, however, he bragged to a deputy sheriff that he was an old boyfriend of Governor Ann Richards and that she would help him out. The guy had indeed been a classmate of Ann's at Waco High School but *not* an old boyfriend. She had definitely not helped him get out of prison. The deputy sheriff turned out to be a Republican, though, and no fan of Ann Richards. As the heat of the campaign intensified, he reminded Bush campaign officials of the prisoner's claim three years earlier. Now heavily embellished, the claim was too juicy a tale for the Bush folks to pass up. They began feverishly spinning a false story that Ann had gotten the prisoner out early and needed to be called to account for his crime.

We had no idea that any of this was going on until we got a call from a Texas newspaper that had picked up the grisly story and wanted a comment prior to publication. We were in the middle of preparation for the first and only debate between the governor and candidate Bush. This kind of sleazy smear was the last thing I wanted to deal with on that particular day. But I could just see the headline: "Governor Charged with Helping to Free Prisoner Who Kills Two Innocent

People." All the Bush campaign needed was a headline that could be used in a dramatic TV ad with ominous music signaling impending danger because of the governor's actions. We knew that we had to stop the phony story however we could.

I immediately left our debate prep to consult with a couple of the state's top libel lawyers to see if we had any legal options to block the story. They told me that we would have to prove "malicious intent" through a court hearing, which we clearly did not have time to do. The attorneys advised me that our best option was "persuasion," not coercion. So, prepped by the lawyers, I politely asked the paper's managing editor, who was a much-respected old-time journalist, to hold back the story until he had detailed facts about the case. After a lengthy conversation, he reluctantly agreed to do so. In the meantime, we found a letter in the governor's correspondence files that included a plea from the prisoner's son to help his father at an upcoming parole hearing. But there was also a notation from Ann to the son, saying that she would not be able to help his father. We sent that along to the newspaper editor, who also learned that the prisoner's early release came about because of the quirky and irresponsible way the Texas Department of Corrections chose to deal with a federal court order to end serious and dangerous overcrowding issues within its prison system. Federal judge William Wayne Justice, after presiding over one of the longest prison lawsuits in the country, issued a court order in 1979, ruling that serious overcrowding and other disturbing actions were resulting in "cruel and unusual punishment" for the prison population and were a violation of the US Constitution. He placed the vast prison system under federal jurisdiction and oversight until Texas could, or would, adequately deal with overcrowding and other critical issues. Texas would have to pay a huge daily fine whenever prison capacity exceeded 95 percent of available beds or space.[3]

Under Republican governor William Clements, who preceded Ann in office, the Texas solution to comply with the court order had been to release big batches of inmates every time the system got close to full capacity. Most of those released were supposed to have been incarcerated because of nonviolent crimes or already eligible for paroles, not yet approved. In June 1991 Ann's old classmate was one of several prisoners eligible for parole who were released early to make room for the newcomers.

The morning after our conversation, the managing editor killed the newspaper story. It never saw the light of day.

While all of this was going on, our staff was so wrapped up in the debate hoopla and its aftermath that few people outside the inner circle of our campaign ever knew about this crisis or a few others just like it. Besides, although we thought Ann performed brilliantly in the debate, Bush made no major gaffes and survived fairly intact, which was all he needed to do in a face-to-face encounter with Ann. He was statesmanlike, and the Texas press loved it. As a result, we came out of the debate and the prisoner release story exhausted and demoralized as we entered the final days of the campaign.

In the overall context of how campaigns operate, it helps to remember that explosive or questionable charges like the prisoner release story rarely come directly from the candidate at the top of the ticket. Plausible deniability is a must-have protection for candidates or officeholders who may or may not know what's going on when their staffs get caught in some unsavory venture. It always helps to claim innocence. Bush never uttered a word about the prisoner story during the final week of the campaign.

Although we were almost always playing a defensive game, it was not as if we did not counterattack and push our own hard-hitting narrative about Bush's failed business ventures. We repeatedly focused on his lack of any kind of leadership experience that would qualify him to be governor as well as his life of privilege that allowed him to escape the consequences of his frequent reckless actions. But to the venerable Texas press corps, with a few exceptions, George W. Bush was the shiny new object that Ann Richards had been only a few years earlier. His charm, pet names, and cheery demeanor won them over. Even with the barrage of our TV ads, we could not make anything stick.

A fundamental rule of political campaigns is that "whoever controls the dialogue controls the outcome." We clearly lost control of the dialogue—the narrative that would tell our story in stark contrast to

Bush's. The election outcome seemed foreordained after we realized that the rural Democratic vote in East Texas was evaporating because of Ann's so-called guns and gays policies. Bush was sweeping the suburbs with his law and order message, and our get-out-the-vote effort among Democratic base voters was lackluster and joyless. We limped across the finish line and lost decisively.

Although I was devastated, Ann actually seemed relieved. She had worked hard at being governor every single day she was in office. Even during the hectic campaign, she often stayed up after midnight in the Governor's Mansion to go through a big stack of policy briefing papers, office details, and agency reports as well as trying to keep up with her voluminous correspondence. The stresses of trying to govern while under constant attack were clearly wearing her down, a fact she tried to hide from all of us. The tension seemed to seep out on election night. After she made her concession call to newly elected Governor Bush and was on her way out the door of our campaign office to greet her supporters in that same ballroom where she had enjoyed her victory four years earlier, she simply gave in to her exhaustion. "I think Bush may have done me a favor tonight, maybe adding a few more years to my life," she whispered.

The Aftermath

It took a lot of time for the shock of our defeat to settle in and for me to learn that what distinguishes a losing campaign from a winning campaign, apart from the obvious and immediate analysis, is how we remember it. Early on, it was the victor's version of our defeat that readily absorbed my attention and guilt. After all, winners always get to write the history, and winning erases most of the mistakes and insanities encompassed in an election victory, while losing always exaggerates them. Because we had allowed ourselves to believe that our "brilliance" created our exhilarating victory in 1990, it would be natural to assume that our "stupidity" produced the disaster of our 1994 loss. If only it were that simple. The truth is always in the mix.

Although ineptitude, poor planning, and major mistakes always contribute to hard-fought campaign losses, demographic and economic conditions can also be a major factor in determining the outcome of most serious political races. When I could become more analytical, rather than emotional, I was more philosophical about our loss. Shifting political winds were sweeping across the country in 1994. Two years into Bill Clinton's presidency, Republicans were proving to be invincible in the midterm congressional elections. Newt Gingrich and an aggressive bunch of young Republican lawmakers took over the US House of Representatives. The Republican sweep also spilled over into statewide elections all over the country. In addition to Ann Richards, even popular New York governor Mario Cuomo lost his seat.[4]

As the months wore on, what ultimately seemed worse to me than the humiliation of losing the campaign was watching helplessly while almost everything we had tried to do during Ann's term was being dismantled piece by piece.

Governor Bush was so genial and likable that few people really noticed how quickly most of Ann's policy initiatives were dropped. Most of the remaining drug or alcohol treatment programs in Texas's vast prison system were simply stopped as an unneeded expense, even though a majority of inmates were either addicted to drugs or had committed drug-related crimes. Fewer inspections of substandard nursing homes took place, and there was virtually no enforcement of safe water or clear air rules. Texas schools were saddled with onerous standardized testing requirements that became the model for Bush's much-disliked "No Child Left Behind" education program after he became president in 2001. Insurance reforms were rolled back, and minority appointments to state boards and commissions were reduced. But Bush was extraordinarily popular, and that popularity swept him into the White House in 2000.

After Bush, the next two governors finished the demolition of the New Texas that Ann had fought so hard to achieve. Governor Rick Perry took a wrecking ball to basic good government practices, and his "pay to play" special-interest politics became a governing philosophy. The next governor, Greg Abbott, was vapid and uninspiring, yet determined to ride the developing right-wing surge, no matter how senseless it proved to be. Within a few short years, Texas had reverted to its most reactionary posturing and foolishness before the reforms of the 1970s and the twenty-year era of moderate, progressive governance that ended with the defeat of Ann Richards in 1994.

Texas has always produced enormous wealth. With few brief exceptions, however, it has always stayed in the hands of its richest citizens, while the middle class has carried the burden of the state's unequal tax policies and the poor have largely been ignored. Texas's governors who followed Ann have reinforced the old structures of power from which the state had struggled to emerge for decades. I finally had to come to terms with my obviously delusional belief that our policies would have a lasting impact once they had been put into place. I learned the hard way that anything that can be "done" in the political world can be swiftly "undone." Our vision of a New Texas was easily demolished and almost completely forgotten within a few short years.

Ann Richards was the last of her kind in twentieth-century Texas. As recently as 2021—thirty years after her election—no other Democrat had been elected to the governor's office. Those of us who were veterans of Ann's glory days continued to hope for a politician with her wit and courage to emerge and take on the extremists who ruled afterward. But the times were different. Texas was different. While Ann was unique for her time, or any other time, I now wonder if our memories are mere reflections of the sun and the moon in the deep well of Texas politics rather than the realities of entrenched political power in our state. I don't think we fully came to terms with the fact that true power resided not in the offices we held but in the corporate boardrooms of big oil, big banking, big insurance, and the other economic behemoths that had never lost their grip. Texas government would continue to serve their interests. We were a temporary irritant and were dealt with accordingly.

Still, most of us carried a stubborn hope into other ventures, holding on to some deeper belief that reason and sanity might ultimately prevail in a political world that still had a hold on us. We moved on. And Ann moved on as well. She was still a national celebrity and

With Ann Richards near the end of her life. We were friends for more than thirty-five years and worked together on numerous projects, both before and after her term as governor ended.

much sought-after speaker. She traveled all over the world and lived in New York for a while, where she had financially rewarding work for Jack Martin's public affairs consulting business. She had a grand time reconnecting with notable Texans who lived in New York, often going to the theater or dinner with columnist Liz Smith and publisher Joe Armstrong, who helped guide her entry into the world of the rich and famous there. Ultimately, she returned home to Texas and immersed herself again in the Austin community she loved. She liked what I was doing at KLRU, Austin's PBS station, and got involved as a board member. And there I was, much to my amazement, "working" for her again—full circle back to our beginning. I never saw that coming!

A Reluctant Ending

Part of what sustained Ann and made her happy with Austin life was her loving relationship with Bud Shrake, a noted sportswriter, novelist, screenwriter, a bit of a mystic, and author of one of the best-selling golf books of all time—*Harvey Penick's Little Red Book*. Ann and Bud had been part of the infamous Mad Dog group of creative, libertine friends in Ann's early, wild drinking days. In their later years, both were divorced, single, and successful and had given up drinking, with many years of sobriety between them. Their love for movies plus their off-the-wall sense of humor and shared history led to a 17-year romance that lasted until Ann died. It was well underway even before she became governor.

In November 1990, after Ann's surprise gubernatorial victory, a small group of us retreated to South Padre Island to begin planning her administration—Jack Martin, Cathy Bonner, Jane Hickie, Paul Williams, Joy Anderson, Bill Cryer, and Ann's long-time assistant Nancy Kohler. Bud Shrake accompanied us and joined us for a meal or two during our few days of intense work. He and Ann would take long walks on the beach when we had afternoon breaks.

On one of those walks, Bud asked Ann if she would be willing to give up politics and the governor's office if he asked her to marry him. "Hell no," she said as they cracked up laughing. When I ran into Bud's son, Ben Shrake, many years later, I told him the story and we laughed again: as Ben said, "You know Dad would never have asked the question if he didn't already know the answer."

Ann's friends loved Bud's sardonic humor and take on politics and life. We were glad that she had such a satisfying relationship as she grew older. But then she got sick. Her last year was spent in and out of M. D. Anderson Cancer Center in Houston for experimental treatments for esophageal cancer. Fortunately, she was able to spend her final few weeks at home, surrounded by her family and closest friends.

I was in the midst of remodeling my new home in Dallas when I got the call from Jane Hickie, letting me know that Ann's life had ended. Like all of us who had been there from the beginning, I rushed to

Austin to help friends and family prepare a huge public tribute to her life. Old friend Jack Martin made it financially possible for us to carry off a grand celebratory event with heartfelt love, music, celebrities, and emotional and humorous tributes with the kind of flair that Ann would have loved.

On the morning of the event, Ann's family and a few of her closest friends gathered for a private burial service at the Texas State Cemetery. Bud Shrake's words touched me more deeply than any other tribute that day.

> We know life is far grander than just chemistry. We are beings of spirit. And even across the divide of death, Ann's spirit remains an echo in our hearts . . . so put a smile on your face, and a good thought in your heart, and try to do the right thing—and you will find Ann standing beside you with a fresh bag of popcorn. Thank you, Ann. I love you.
> Ah-men . . . Ah-women . . . Ah-Ann.[5]

Ah-Ann, indeed.

My life was so much richer for being part of hers. I felt a profound sense of loss that day, as did so many of us who had been lucky enough to have shared parts of her remarkable journey through life and politics.

Shortly after Ann's death, I turned down an offer to write her biography because I felt I knew too much, cared too much, and on some level felt that I still needed to protect her image and her legacy. Like most of us in politics, Ann hid her vulnerabilities and never wanted to reveal the hurt she felt while under constant attack. I also never wanted to reveal anything that might bring more hurt to her family and closest friends. Some bonds of friendship remain even after death.

Although I didn't quite realize it at the time, Ann's death was truly the end of my intensive and visible role in a progressive movement in Texas. It had started with my husband, John Rogers, and ended with Ann Richards. But its roots went far deeper and were much farther away.

PART II

The Personal Is Political

Sicily

Although I am only half Sicilian—note that I say Sicilian instead of Italian—I have at times alternately rejected and embraced a Sicilian spirit as I have tried to understand all that is hidden in our lives.

That spirit is a skeptical attitude toward life and a guide to participating in it, rooted in a culture where dangerous power could shape your destiny. In the Sicily of my ancestors, danger could be found among the wealthy landowners, in the halls of government offices, within the church, in the harsh weather cycles, or in bitter rivalries among neighbors and families and even within the body itself, with its hidden weaknesses and uncontrollable passions. And, of course, the sinister presence of the Mafia permeated everything. That was reality. It was political and intensely personal.

How did that spirit extend across continents and vast bodies of waters and take root in my consciousness as I was growing up in Dallas, Texas?

Did that spirit help or hinder me as I was lured into the raucous world of Texas politics? And why did that genetic skepticism take so long to kick in and break apart my illusions?

MY FATHER TOOK A PHOTO of me on Easter Sunday when I was about ten years old. There I was, too tall for my age but so proud of my two-piece red gabardine suit, my white straw hat, and the white plastic purse on my arm. I was on my way to be baptized—sprinkled—into the little neighborhood Methodist church my mother favored, rather than the Catholic parish I sometimes attended with my father's Sicilian family.

When I look at that photo now, I see a goofy little girl with a crooked smile who thought she was a grown-up. Yet even now I am not sure if my pivotal action that day was about religion or a desire to break from

In 1902 Bernardo (Ben) Coniglio left Sicily to settle in Dallas, Texas. A year later, he married Mary Palumbo, who was born in Houston into a family from Ben's home village of Corleone, outside of Palermo. He and Mary raised four children, including Frank Coniglio, my father.

one culture and immerse myself into another. Whatever it was, I know that it required an inner weighing or at least some sort of mulling over that might have been possible only because my child's brain had developed enough neurons to open a portal to an inner consciousness that led to an emergent sense of self. But it was still a child's brain—not yet conscious enough to know what my roots were or that I had already absorbed the Sicilian spirit of my father.

It took me years to learn that my ancestors, the old Sicilians of the Mezzogiorno,[1] which historians have called the land that time forgot, intuitively understood that things were rarely as they appeared to be and that a search for truth might bring peril.

Their spirit was encompassed in the novels of Leonardo Sciascia, one of Italy's most popular post–World War II writers, who created tales of Sicilian village life where innocents were destroyed when they foolishly tried to discover the reasons for actions taken by landowners or the church or local magistrates or the cause of a suspicious accident that befell someone who displeased the local *capo* (boss). So, for the most part, they didn't bother to look and merely shrugged their shoulders or rolled their eyes silently as if to say, "Well, whatcha gonna do?" Novelist Sciascia understood that Sicilian fear and skepticism also served as a kind of moral inoculation against entrapment by overwhelming and corruptible power.

Maybe this moral inoculation against entrapment was genetic and actually helped me navigate the perils of the political world in which my public life has been immersed. Perhaps the Sicilian spirit and skepticism became an enhancement in my life. After all, as Sciascia has written, "Skepticism isn't an acceptance of defeat, but a margin of safety, or elasticity . . . the best antidote to fanaticism."[2]

La Famiglia

I grew up in the midst of a Sicilian family that settled in Dallas, the place of my birth. They never talked much about the old country; nor did they identify themselves primarily as Sicilian. Even mainland Italians looked down on the Sicilian peasants, with their mixture of folk taboos, fears, and superstitions, not to mention their darker mix of Arab, Greek, and African blood. When they came to America, the Sicilian immigrants were at the lowest level of the hierarchy of foreign hatreds. But mainland Italian immigrants did not fare much better. My grandfather so desired assimilation that he never wanted his children to speak the Sicilian dialect or even basic Italian. He was resourceful enough to build several successful businesses, was one of the founders of a weekly newspaper that served the Italian community, and became a respected elder among Dallas's Sicilian families. My father, my aunts, and their contemporaries who were born here became American to the core. Or so I thought.

I once made a list of Sicilian instructions that shaped me in ways that I have only recently understood. Now I know that they were rooted in the peasant countryside where La Cosa Nostra struck fear in every heart. Or perhaps it was Sicilian culture itself, forged through thousands of years of invasions, occupation, betrayal, extortion, and violence, where the Mafia once offered pricy protection from the invasive forces of church and state. Maybe it was just my father's family, whose central purpose seemed to be to stay out of harm's way. It was better to accept your situation and stay hidden rather than challenge or question the stronger forces that surrounded you. Only later, when I came across an old Mafia saying, "The best word is the one not spoken," did I come to understand my own inner conflicts. My father had unwittingly taught me Sicilian rules of survival:

> Don't call attention to yourself.
> Don't brag about your achievements.
> Don't let anyone see your weaknesses or vulnerabilities.
> Don't ask for help without knowing you will pay a price.
> Don't trust anyone outside the immediate family.
> Don't take risks.

Most importantly, mind your own business and don't ask too many questions. My father seemed guided by another old Sicilian expression: "A man who looks for reasons finds thorns as well as roses." Sciascia explored this unique Sicilian truth in his novels. All of his characters who searched too deeply for hidden truths—and let themselves be seen in the process—were ripped apart by the thorns they found along the way. So I force myself to tread lightly.

Even with all of these Sicilian prohibitions, my childhood in Dallas was not without simple family-based pleasures: lots of good food and practical jokes at big family dinners; a little taste of sweet red wine if you wanted what the adults were drinking; operettas under the stars at the Fair Park Band Shell; Sunday mornings with my dad in the appliance shop of his boyhood friend who was called "Radio Sam" because he was such an electronic wizard. I loved the heightened excitement of being with all my cousins on Christmas Eve or on summer evenings, chasing fireflies across family lawns filled with fig trees and rose arbors, thorns and all.

La Americana

The rub was always that my beautiful mother wanted more: shoes from Neiman Marcus, dancing and piano lessons for her girls, magazines and books, movies on Sunday afternoon, a night out every now and then without the kids.

My mother was "La Americana," initially not a welcome member of the Sicilian family. My father's three sisters and his mother feared that letting a non-Italian, non-Catholic into the family would somehow break the familial bond and bring disapproval from the small, close-knit Dallas Sicilian community, where most members were connected by various degrees of family or village relationships. But my dad was headstrong and deeply in love with my mother, a smart Scots-Irish high-school girl from East Texas who came to Dallas to work during the Great Depression. My dad was the "baby" and my grandfather's only son, so the old man insisted that the women of his family treat my mother with respect. My dad, Frank Coniglio, got his way and married Saletha Anita Hicks. Yet he ended up being caught between two worlds: his culture and Catholic upbringing and her assertiveness and East Texas Social Gospel Methodism. It was not easy for either of them.

Now I know that I was equally caught between their worlds.

Like most children, I didn't have any sense of being Italian or being different until one jarring summer afternoon when I was seven or eight years old. Our East Dallas neighborhood gaggle of kids played together almost every day. On this particular day, my younger sister Martha and I had drifted down to little Billy Boedecker's yard, where a minor fistfight broke out among a couple of the boys. Billy was obviously getting the worst of it, so his mother ran out of the house to break up the fight, pulling the boys off her son. She shooed all the kids out of her yard then looked at Martha and me and shouted, "Get out of my yard,

In 1939 Frank Coniglio married Anita Hicks, who grew up in a Scots-Irish family in East Texas. Here they are with me (their first child), when I was about a year old.

you dirty little dagos!" Martha and I ran all the way home. We didn't know why we were singled out or what Mrs. Boedecker meant, but we were upset and told our mother what had happened. Our brave little non-Italian mother, La Americana, rushed down to Mrs. Boedecker's house, pounded on her door, and told her in no uncertain words never to insult her children again. And she didn't. But Martha and I avoided her yard and little Billy too. From that point on, I knew that we were different, outsiders in some way, and that an unpronounceable name ending in a vowel or your skin color or your religion could determine how people looked at you and assessed your worth or lack thereof.

Something else marked me as well. Both of my parents had strong empathy for those who had been unfairly treated by life. Even while wearing her Neiman Marcus shoes, my mother remembered the bitter days of the Depression in East Texas, where her mother had to stand in line to get surplus food commodities to feed her six children. Unlike many Southern white people, she had an early awakening to the rightness of the civil rights movement and valued Franklin Delano Roosevelt's New Deal. Although my dad was far less willing to express himself publicly, he felt that way too. He was a confirmed Democrat, primarily because the party had nominated Catholic Al Smith for president in 1928. Their common interest in politics, albeit from different perspectives, engendered the same affliction in me.

I remember a night drive when we were returning from a family vacation in New Orleans. I was still awake in the back seat while my little sisters were sleeping and my parents were listening to a radio broadcast of the goings-on at the 1952 Democratic National Convention that selected Adlai Stevenson as its nominee. Somehow the excitement of the process reached me through those radio waves. I was as glued to the static-filled broadcast as were my parents.

The feeling I had that night was reinforced several years later when my parents took me to one of those raucous neighborhood precinct meetings where the liberals and conservatives vied for control of the Texas Democratic Party. By happenchance we lived only a few blocks but millions of dollars away from the legendary oil tycoon H. L. Hunt. His massive home, a replica of Mount Vernon, stood majestically on a hill above Dallas's White Rock Lake. Hunt funded the John Birch Society, the right-wing Freedom Forum, and radio talk shows that paved the way for the likes of Rush Limbaugh and even Alex Jones in the Donald Trump years. And lo and behold, H. L. Hunt and his entourage showed up at our neighborhood precinct meeting. I got to see up close and personal the richest, most famous right-wing extremist in America. His fat, pinkish skin reflected an almost evil malevolence to me that night. He had come to the precinct hustings to fight the loyalist Democrats in their perennial unsuccessful battle to wrest control of the state's Democratic Party from the ultraconservative and all-powerful moguls who controlled the levers of political power in Texas. As usual, my parents' hearty band of liberal neighbors lost. But the battle seemed fun and interesting in a grown-up way for the earnest adolescent I was becoming, and I fed on my parents' breakfast conversations about the political news of the day.

While my parents would do their civic duty and show up at the neighborhood meetings, that was about the extent of their common political activism. My mother was willing to take risks by speaking out on social and political issues. My father feared the consequences and felt that he needed to "protect" her from her own altruistic impulses. Of course, she wanted no protection from what she believed to be right action. I absorbed the tension between them and internalized their conflicting views of the world. Was it my duty to challenge a hostile world or to follow the Sicilian rules for survival? Now I realize that this tension was probably one of the sources of the ambivalence I sometimes felt while engaging in public action. Yet, even within the conflict about "how," I had no conflict about "what." My sense of politics emerged from my parents' beliefs—Democratic . . . liberal . . . activist . . . empathetic. How could it be any other way? My mother had experienced poverty, and my father had known discrimination. They both felt that it was the intervention of a benevolent government that helped them along the way. Each instilled in me a firm conviction of the need for fair treatment for those who were on the edge of life's currents and did not have "advantages." But it would be many years before I had the curiosity to link my beliefs and actions to the underlying tensions of two different cultures.

Diving into the Sicilian Well

A few years ago, I was able to travel to Sicily with two of my sisters, Martha Coniglio and Susie Calmes. We wanted to learn about the lives of our ancestors.[3] But we hardly knew where to begin. We were tourists captivated by some mysterious force that had a hold on us. Each Sicilian experience resulted in a surprise, a jolt of recognition, a glimpse of incomparable beauty, or a stab of fear, sometimes all at the same time.

First, there was the surprise of Palermo's beauty—the *Trinacria* of land, sea, and mountains; the magical light; the sensuous delight of its old neighborhoods full of flowers and food stalls; the visual reminders of complex Greek and Arab influences through the ages.[4] No one in our family had ever told us about this. The surprises continued. One day we had a chance encounter with primitive pageantry when we first heard the mournful music of a brass band and saw a traditional Good Friday procession of parishioners spilling out of a nondescript church. They were costumed as Roman soldiers leading a penitent young man dressed as Jesus. He carried a cross and wore a crown of thorns. Two dozen young men dressed in tuxedos followed him, carrying on their shoulders a wooden platform holding a massive black velvet-clad statue of the grieving Virgin Mary. The traditional Sicilian spectacle was macabre, yet moving in some inexplicable way. What fascinated me most, however, were the jostling crowds of simply dressed people lining the narrow streets, who gasped and made the sign of the cross as the parade moved past them. I watched the faces in the crowd—many matched my own and those of my family: My Uncle John's nose, Aunt Rosie's full red lips, Uncle Tony's hooded eyes, my father's rounded cheeks. A few of those faces even framed pale blue eyes like my grandmother's, the result of some residual gene left among the natives by the Norman invaders more than a thousand years ago. All of these faces were so familiar, yet so different.

Corleone

In Corleone, the birthplace of La Cosa Nostra as well as of my grandfather, Bernardo Maria Coniglio, we felt another surprising jolt of recognition, as if some genetic memory had been awakened. We felt an inexplicable ache in our hearts for the old ones, particularly when we walked through the cemetery and saw the headstones of so many families whose names we knew as children: Grazaffi, Listi, Dragna, Genarro, Piccolo, LaBarba, and of course at least a half-dozen Coniglio grave markers. Our history was there in that ancient graveyard.

It was in Sicilian villages like Corleone that Giuseppe Garibaldi gathered his foot soldiers in 1860 to take the mainland and unite Italy.

His dream of democracy failed when the new unified government in Rome took the Sicilian land of the Bourbon conquerors and gave it to the church instead of to the peasants who had worked it for centuries. And it was from those villages that hundreds of Corleonesi young men and their wives, children, and sisters fled to the United States from 1890 to 1920 with hope for more than they would ever know at home. My grandfather, two of his brothers, and an older sister were among them.

Corleone had emerged from the thirteenth century as a market center in this rural area. The town is built around a small piazza that serves as the radius from which narrow cobblestone streets lead in all directions, some meandering up the stony mountains, and others sloping down into the Corleone River valley. Corleone means "heart of the lion." Strong, brave, fierce. The town was immortalized in *The Godfather*. Small numbers of tourists make the drive along mountain roads from Palermo each year to taste the atmosphere of movie crime. But organized crime was not a movie fantasy for Corleone. Only a few months before we arrived, Italian anti-Mafia police finally captured Bernardo Provenzano, the "Phantom of Corleone" and the real godfather of La Cosa Nostra. Provenzano had been a fugitive for forty years, living most of that time in a little hut in the hills on the outskirts of Corleone. He was one of the most powerful men in Italy, and the crime tentacles of his Corleone family and friends had reached the national government in Rome and all the way into the streets of the United States. Provenzano eschewed modern technology to issue instructions to his far-flung organization in tiny handwritten coded notes smuggled in his Bible. He had been found when police followed a delivery boy on a bicycle bringing Provenzano a bundle of clean clothes, carefully laundered by his wife in Corleone.

None of that was on our minds when we ate lunch at Corleone's chief hotel, Leon d'Oro, located on a steep hill a mile or so from the piazza. The hotel was surrounded by a grove of trees known as prayer trees because their berries were so hard and round that they had once been used to make rosary beads. The hotel dining room had a simple charm. We sat at a table next to an afternoon feast set up for about twenty members of the owner's family. The familiar names in the cemetery and the family-style dinner in this little hotel evoked the comfort of all my childhood dinners with aunts and uncles and cousins, reminding me of the sweet excesses of big Italian all-day weddings and dances; the organized silliness of bunko parties that my aunt held for the Sicilian ladies; the visits to several St. Joseph's Tables over the course of an evening, set up in Sicilian homes with food and pastries to give thanks for answered prayers; and the visits to Zia Anna, my grandfather's older sister, who was the first of his family to come to America and the last to die. These and all of the other long-buried memories of immersion in my father's Sicilian family flooded over me. I felt a strange and surprising serenity in this place.

Now I know that I probably romanticized the experience of Sicily. After all, for centuries it had been a haven for poverty, corruption, brutality, fear, and superstition. My grandfather Bernardo (Ben) had to leave his village and family behind to have a life of hope and promise. Perhaps the Sicily of my imagination, with all of its beauty and charm, was one more illusion that I carried with me into life. Yet I also know that growing up in an Americanized Sicilian culture shaped me in ways that I struggled for years to understand.

After I returned home, I read Peter Robb's labyrinthine tale of the Sicilian mafia, *Midnight in Sicily*.[5] It is a marvelous history of Sicily from the end of World War II through the mid-1990s, when it became public that the wave of Mafia killings and corruption reached into the highest levels of the Christian Democratic Party that had ruled Italy since the end of World War II. The worldwide Mafia had been dominated since the 1940s by the Corleonesi mob, once led by brutal and brilliant Toto Riina. It had been centralized, connected, and controlled by Riina, his Corleonesi relatives, and associates like his successor, Provenzano. When Robb went to Corleone for research on his book, he sat in the same central piazza, saw the same prayer trees, and walked through the same village cemetery, just as we had done. He noted the empty streets and crumbling buildings and came away with a feeling of oppression and a sense of the sinister.

In contrast, fifteen years later, I came away with a sense of wonder and nostalgia. We were looking for different things and each found what we wanted. I saw the sun and the moon reflected in novelist Sciascia's metaphorical well. As a historian, Robb jumped in and saw the truth. And that is the reality of Sicily: we find only what we want to see. For a very long time, that was the reality of Texas politics for me. I saw what I most wanted to see.

Even today, when I let myself get close to the well of truth that Sciascia described, I seem only to be discovering one more Sicilian surprise when the light of the sun and the peace of the moon reflected in the still waters are washed away: *there are no clear-cut answers to anything.* The hard truths I was seeking often seemed to be as elusive as the summer fireflies I chased when I was a child. Their glowing light-bursts led only deeper into the darkness, where I always seemed to lose the light just before I could grasp it.

All of the old Sicilian immigrants of my childhood are gone now, as are their second-generation children like my father and his sisters. Even people of my generation have been assimilated or are dying off, and the Sicilian aphorisms have been overrun and absorbed in an American pop culture that negates each one of them. But I have learned that my inner psyche was shaped by those Sicilian fears. They extended my differences and outsider psychology far more than did my unpronounceable name. I always held back, observed, and sized up a situation carefully before I made a move. I was afraid to speak out or make my voice heard, even though I had strong opinions and marketable skills. I was almost forty years old before I ever made a public speech or took on a leadership role for a cause that was important to me—and that was only because the indomitable Ann Richards made me do it. Harm did not come, at least not then. When it did, it had nothing to do with politics or Sicily or the outer world that I so loved.

The Hard Box

My first hint of what awaited came from the man sitting across from us in the admitting area. He was wearing a face mask, skewed in a way that caused my eyes to linger longer than they should. But I turned away quickly when I realized why: there was no protrusion in the center of his face to hold the mask in place. The man had no nose.

I squeezed John's hand, hoping he had not noticed. I wanted to shield his eyes and his gauze-shrouded head, still mummy-wrapped from the exploratory surgery only a few days earlier. In that moment, I felt more like his mother than his wife, holding tightly in my lap the brown padded envelope that contained a lipstick-sized plastic capsule that contained his tumor-tissue.

Four days later, after a battery of tests, scans, and probes, John's team of doctors told us they thought that they could save his life. The price he would pay would be removal of his ear, necessary to reach the malignancy in the ear canal. A side effect of the surgery would be loss of the main facial nerve. There would be other losses as well: muscle from the shoulder would be used to replace the part of the skull to be removed to reach the tumor; skin from the thigh would cover the remaining wound on the head; radiation would be directed at the wound; plastic surgery might be used to rebuild a portion of the face; then, perhaps a year to eighteen months later, a prosthesis could be made to replace the outer ear.

John was stunned. Speechless. So was I. We simply looked at each other across the examining room, slumping in our plastic chairs from the weight of . . . it.

I AM FAR, FAR AWAY from that time and place and the almost daily traumatic events that engulfed us during the first year of John's illness. Yet that place—M. D. Anderson Cancer Hospital and Tumor Institute in Houston, Texas—was as deeply rooted in Texas politics as anything else I encountered along the way.

73

After the first round of tests and probes, John's doctor, a handsome Chilean of German descent, told John that his mind would be unaffected by the eight-hour operation, even though the cancer was growing rapidly from the ear canal back to the base of the brain.

"You can still think and you can still work, but you won't be very pretty," he said.

I think I recovered first, asking the doctor if there was an alternative to such radical surgery. His reply was direct.

"Death in two or three months . . . and it will not be easy or clean because of the location and nature of the tumor."

Then, with real empathy, the first he had shown, he patted John's hand and in his heavy, authoritative accent said, "I'm sorry, my friend. You are caught between the rock and the hard box."

The doctor told John that he had the weekend to decide what he wanted to do. He instructed us to let him know on Monday if we wanted to schedule the surgery or plan for a local referral and a supply of morphine to see John to the end.

We lived that weekend between the rock and the hard box. We had not told anyone of the extremity of the prognosis or the treatment—not even our children, now both in college and away from home at the time. It was not our nature to be self-revealing or to ask for help from anyone. We treasured being independent and on our own—until then, quite happily so. Silent strength and stoicism were our ideals.

I felt the decision to live or to die had to be John's, not mine. As we talked and fell silent together that weekend, I vowed I would put no pressure on him and would support whatever he wanted to do.

John was an asthmatic who had lived his entire life with the muscle fear of not getting enough air to breathe. A doctor had told his parents that he would not survive his fifth year. He believed that he had lived his whole life on borrowed time. Now forty-seven years old, John had little desire for some romantic and valiant last fight against cancer. He was already tired of medicines, emergency rooms, and all-night vigils to push air in and out of his lungs. That weekend he wanted no more of any of it. His solution was to go off to a cabin in the mountains. There he would rest, take his morphine, and die. Okay, I said.

Then on Sunday evening, in our exhausted, now mindless state, we were sitting close together on the couch, ostensibly watching television. We held hands. Our feet were intertwined on the ottoman in front of us. I felt myself sinking into the comfort of his body and the unity of the moment. I did not recognize the pleading tone of my own voice when I whispered, "I don't want you to die."

Stoicism failed each of us that August night. Neither of us was strong enough to go it alone. The next morning John called the hospital and scheduled the operation.

The Power of Place

We made the choice to be at M. D. Anderson Hospital in Houston for my husband's surgery and cancer treatment, which leads to another political tale. But politics was not on our minds for most of the four years that we spent in the hospital's buildings—for weeks at a time during the first year and then for regular visits, tests, other surgeries, consultations, and treatments. It was only later that I came to understand the politics at the very foundation of the hospital's beginnings and mission. At the time, it was only within this community of suffering that we truly felt at home, where John was not looked upon by strangers as a physical pariah and I was not pitied as some long-suffering wife. Here we were simply who we were—a sick man and a well woman struggling with the effects of body cells out of control.

John almost did not make it through his eight-hour surgery to remove the tumor. He suffered a major asthma attack during the procedure, which had to be delayed until his breathing could be regulated. My mother had flown in from Dallas to be with me during the surgery, as had our friends from Austin, Jack and Patsy Martin and Buddy and Ellen Temple. I'm not sure I could have made it through that day without them. Our children, Billy and Eleanor, also stayed with me in Houston at various times during the three weeks we waited for John to recover from the debilitating surgery to go back home to Austin. We needed to be together during this crisis in our lives. At the time, there was no place better for us to be in Texas—or the country—than at M. D. Anderson Cancer Hospital.

Cancer is egalitarian in its essence. And so, at the time, was the quality of treatment at this unique cancer center. From top to bottom, the whole hospital community was focused on innovation and excellence and fostered an amazing institutional kindness in its treatment of men, women, and children of all races—rich or poor—who were struggling to survive their unlucky encounters with the "emperor of all maladies."[1]

Once a janitor put down his mop and took John and me to the X-ray room when we had lost our way to treatment in the maze of corridors. A patient care specialist found me an inexpensive room in the hotel owned by the hospital for outpatients and families. John's young female radiologist worried about his emotional state and spent extra time talking poetry and politics with him. A nutritionist gave John protein supplements to keep his weight up. A surgical intern taught me to care for John's skin graft and bragged on my fearful and inept attempts to follow his precise instructions.

This was not a happy community or one that you wanted to become a part of or even to remain within. It was just that once you were inducted into it and given a number, you began to accept that you were part of it. You settled into being yourself, a self with one tumor or many, or none if you were a bystander like me, but still fighting a fight you did not choose.

Away from that community of suffering and healing, life could take on a very different tone, particularly if you left its safety with some sort of permanent disability that limited movement or control or in John's case an obvious facial disfigurement caused by the extremity of his surgery.

There are 44 muscles in the face, and they are capable of arranging more than 7,000 different expressions. How many expressions did John lose when they removed his ear, leaving the right half of his face in a permanent paralysis? It was impossible to know the number, but so many were clearly visible to the naked eye: the dropped cheek, the drooping eyelid, the downward curl of his once full lips. Laughter, when it came, contorted his face, twisting it up and down at the same time. At first he would not laugh, or when he did he would cover his mouth. Later he did not care. Only his eyes could really register how he felt. They could not lie. Sometimes they emitted the soul-crushing deadness of pain that was unfocused, unseeing, turned inward, away from the world.

I read everything I could find about facial disfigurement and its psychological impact. I wanted to help, but the best I could do was to gently massage the tight muscles in his neck and shoulders every night, as we sat together on that couch where the decision had been made to stay alive. And those times did help in some ways. The emotional closeness of our early days together intensified. What in the world was worth arguing about?

Somehow John came to peace with all of this—the disfigurement, the limited energy, the constant facial pain from so many severed nerve endings, and the ever-increasing asthma attacks, brought on by the simple stresses of living with pain and a debilitating injury. His peace came through work. He wanted to think and focus on ways for his causes to be victorious. Yet he was philosophical about politics as well.

John's friend and coworker Willie Chapman remembered how John reacted after a particularly harsh defeat on some labor-union issue when they were both working for the Texas AFL-CIO (American Federation of Labor and Congress of Industrial Organizations). Willie was devastated, and John asked him why he was so upset. "Well, hell, John," he argued. "We just got the shit kicked out of us. Why do you think I'm upset?" John calmly reassured him: "Willie, you just don't get it. We're not gonna win every time. Our job is to point out the changes that need to be made and every once in a while one of those guys who wins will listen to us and do something about it. So we don't have time to get discouraged. We just have to keep yelling!"

John had figured out what so many of us rarely do: winning is not always what makes a person a hero. It is making common cause with the powerless in pursuit of a worthy cause when you know you may not win but the purpose is worth pursuing. And that's what John did:

he kept on yelling and fighting for workers' rights until the moment he died four years later, totally exhausted from one of those asthma attacks I so feared.

Until the cancer time, I was restless, excitedly rushing through my life but oblivious to some of the realities we might face. We had our precious children, we had our ups and downs, and we had our common political life. Politics and our children were the bonds that held us together. And then it was cancer.

Now, in the decades since his death, I hope that I have not been as oblivious, yet I know that I am not always fully aware either. I grow old. I watch my middle-aged children deal with life's beauties and burdens, some of them life-threatening. My beautiful daughter has had her own devastating experiences with cancer, the scourge of our times, and all I could do was try to be a loving helper. Anyone who has cancer knows what those who have never experienced it do not. I could only be a witness to the suffering of two of the people I loved most dearly. However, it was John Rogers's cancer experience that was at the dead center of the private life I led while floundering in the deep well of Texas politics. And therein is one more political tale.

Politics, Power, and Life

The fight for life is always immediate, individual, and personal. But the fight for an institution like M. D. Anderson, which can assist your fight for life, is impersonal, political, distant, long-range, and removed, if not remote, from the suffering. As an institution, the hospital is engaged in research, technology, fundraising, insurance, administration, and, of course, the maintenance of buildings and bureaucracies. M. D. Anderson Cancer Center grew out of the interplay of politics, policy, and power.

Federal programs, federal initiatives, federal interference, federal regulations, and federal tax dollars originally made the institution—and the community within it—possible. The Hill-Burton Hospital Survey and Construction Act in 1946 made money available through the states to assist local communities build hospitals in return for a pledge in perpetuity to turn no one away because of inability to pay. M. D. Anderson in Houston, Texas, was one of the first beneficiaries of the money. John Rogers was among the thousands of beneficiaries of its care.

The original bipartisan Hill-Burton legislation was one of the most effective bills ever passed by the Congress. It was only nine pages long and contained a simple hypothesis: the construction of new facilities would be stimulated if the federal government provided seed money to spur public and nonprofit hospital construction and attached very few strings to the allocation of the money other than the commitment to serve indigent patients.[2] People who needed hospital care could get it—even poor people. Although John and I were among the fortunate who had health insurance and could pay for what insurance did not, we were still beneficiaries of the advanced research and technology that this unique institution offered to all.

Well . . . John Rogers died anyway. There are time limits to being human, made particularly devastating when illness or disaster shortens the life we hoped we would have. We learned the hard way that even the best institutions cannot always save us. Yet government-initiated and government-directed institutions can create an environment that provides assistance and comfort when we have to deal with the inevitability of aging, illness, accidents, pain, or death. It takes power to create and sustain these public institutions that care for us in times of need, and our democratic society depends on them. I am grateful that during our time there M. D. Anderson continued to adhere to its original mandate to serve all, regardless of the ability to pay.

In the spring of 1995, when he was governor of Texas, George W. Bush—the man who defeated Ann Richards and dismantled most of her programs—signed a law that denied indigent patients free treatment at M. D. Anderson Cancer Center if they could get less specialized treatment in their local hospitals, often only in emergency rooms. This changed M. D. Anderson's fifty-year-old policy of giving equal care to indigent and paying patients, as it had committed to do when it qualified for Hill-Burton federal funds in 1946. While the level of its cancer research and treatment remained the finest in the nation, it was no longer available to all who walked through its doors without personal wealth or a high-priced health insurance policy that could pay the bills. In that aspect, M. D. Anderson became more like any other American hospital: you—or your insurance company—had to pay to play, and you would have to run an obstacle course to find the kinds of extraordinary care you desperately needed. The rationale for the legislative change was that it was costing M. D. Anderson approximately $200 million to treat indigent patients in 1994, compared to $35 million in 1985, when John was still undergoing treatment there. While the numbers of patients had slowly increased, it was the ballooning administrative, technology, and equipment costs that drove the rise in expenditures. Neither the governor nor members of the Texas legislature made the effort to find and allocate additional state funds to deal with increasing costs in order to adhere to the original mandate and mission of the hospital. They simply changed the mandate. Texas walked away from its original agreement with the federal government that allowed the hospital to exist in the first place.

I recount the story of my husband's treatment at M. D. Anderson Hospital not only because it was so significant personally for our family but because it is one of those private stories that somehow hold it all together for me—family, love, health, politics, policy, idealism, and my engagement in the larger world. To know why and how John and I managed our lives during those four difficult years in and out of one of the nation's premier hospitals, I have to go back to our improbable beginning—two shy loners who somehow awkwardly found each other and built a life together centered around family, politics, and a world we wanted to fully experience.

Mr. and Mrs. Extremo

We had only been married for a few weeks when a colorful old San Antonio gambler named Red Berry ran for the state legislature because he wanted to legalize horse racing in Texas. He would buy thirty minutes of television airtime to run old films of big horse races like the Kentucky Derby, the Preakness, and others. He would always end his show with a pitch for votes. The "political" spots were a hoot, the talk of the town. By the end of his campaign, everyone in San Antonio knew about Red Berry, who got himself elected to the Texas legislature.

We didn't own a television set, so we would head to our neighborhood bar to watch his shows. When my very traditional Sicilian father found out that his daughter was hanging out in bars with her radical husband to watch TV, he bought us a television set and drove from Dallas to San Antonio to bring it to us.

We sent Red Berry a note of congratulations and thanked him for his role in helping us get a TV set.[1] That was the fun side of politics. As it turned out, it was also a good way to kick off a 27-year relationship that expanded our horizons and changed our lives.

WHEN WE MET ON MY night shift at the *Daily Texan*, I was a 19-year-old college junior eager to become a journalist and writer and John was a 25-year-old copy editor at the *San Antonio Light*. The *Daily Texan* was the heralded student newspaper at the University of Texas in Austin that served as training ground for many of the nation's top journalists, including Walter Cronkite and Bill Moyers.[2] John had dropped out of the university halfway through his senior year to work at the *Light* so that he could provide financial support for his sister's entry into college and help his mother and two younger brothers at home. His father had been ill and unable to work, and his mother was a special-education

teacher in the San Antonio public schools. When Bertie—Sis—graduated from college and became a teacher like her mother, John was
free to continue his education. Although he moved back to Austin, he
continued to work at the *San Antonio Light* on the weekends.

I was a night editor on the *Texan*, which was still reeling from the
controversial tenure of the legendary student editor Willie Morris, who
had alienated university administrators and the Texas legislature with
his scathing editorials against segregation, censorship, and the state's
official collusion with oil and gas interests.[3] On my nights as editor, I
usually selected the contents for the news section of the paper, edited
the stories, and prepared the layout. The paper would be distributed
seven days a week on campus and all across Austin.

Our night staff was small: a few reporters finishing up their stories,
the sports editor and his team, and a few copy editors who wrote headlines and fact-checked the articles. We were all impressed when this old
guy—and that is how we thought of John at the time—started dropping
by sometimes to write a few headlines and read the news wires. He
had worked on the *Texan* with Willie Morris. He was quick and craggy,
often pulling stories off the Associated Press (AP) wire that many of us
would not have noticed. After all, he was a "grown-up" who had been
out in the world. I was a little intimidated by this man who was alternately skeptical and silent. In the beginning, he rarely had more than a
few words to say to me. But he watched. I knew he watched.

In the old days of the newspaper world—before computers and
technology changed the business of news—we put the paper to bed on
the editorial side and sent our stacks of copy paper to the print shop.
Then they had to be typeset by the Linotype operators in the basement
of the journalism building. As night editor, I had to approve the final
typeset markup before the press run. It took a couple of hours from the
time we sent the copy to the pressroom before the paper was ready for
my final read. I'd usually clean up the mess on the news desk and maybe
read an assignment for another class or just hang out until the paper
was ready to be proofed, usually around midnight on a good night.

I was startled one night when John asked me to go for coffee with
him while I waited for the call from the pressroom. At the time, there

was only one late night diner open in downtown Austin, and he drove us there in his Ford Thunderbird.

So it started with talk on our occasional late-night forays . . . lots of talk and black coffee. I can't even remember what we talked about then, probably the news, or how brave *Daily Texan* editor Willie Morris had been to call out the evils of segregation in Texas. I was already interested in politics, so I'm sure I babbled on about the young senator John Kennedy, who looked like he might run for president. I do remember that John began to tease me about my infatuation with "Junior" Kennedy, but I wasn't sure if our relationship was a friendship or a budding romance. Sometimes I thought he liked me. Sometimes I was sure he didn't. But he came to see me in Dallas on New Year's Eve. We had a real date—dress-up clothes and all the trimmings.

We attended one of those big downtown hotel New Year's Eve extravaganzas, with dinner and dancing, confetti and balloons at midnight. We were both miserable. I was certain that this date would end whatever we thought was going on between us. However, the next day we braved the frigid weather to attend the annual New Year's Cotton Bowl game. The all-white Texas football team got swamped by the top team in the country, Syracuse, whose Black players had been taunted by some of Texas's good old white boys. It was not pleasant. But the mood shifted later that evening when we saw the Broadway touring company of *My Fair Lady* at the Fair Park Music Hall. Something about our mixed experiences that weekend shifted everything between us. Was it the evidence of some sort of compatibility? Although we both loved Texas football, we were mortified by the racist sneers from the Texas crowd. But that evening we discovered that the clever staging and musicality of Broadway shows could captivate our attention and imagination. Perhaps more importantly, we both absolutely hated the forced holiday joviality among strangers in some celebratory ballroom. Maybe that New Year's experience was simply the first time that either of us could imagine the possibility of a common life with someone who would indulge our love of news and politics and share our skepticism about anything that seemed too conventional or phony.

I was fully committed to a future with John by Valentine's Day, after he told me, "I fell in love with your writing even before I knew you." What girl can resist a line like that? And I didn't. I believed him because everything about this strange man was genuine. He was a no-bullshit, quirky kind of a guy. No false sentimentality. No "put-on" phony airs. No pet names. No superficial compliments—at least most of the time. It took a while for reality to replace romanticism when I finally realized that it was not my clever turn of phrase that he loved but the topic of one of my stories.

I had written a long piece for the *Daily Texan* about the Texas legislature's anti-labor laws that restricted the rights of workers to organize and bargain collectively. Accompanying the article was a cartoon of a legislator's oversized boot stomping down on a hapless worker. I had been thrilled when Texas liberal US senator Ralph Yarborough picked up the piece and inserted it into the Congressional Record. Years later, when John began to work for the Texas AFL-CIO to protect the rights of the workers I had described, we came full circle back to the issue that had sparked our lifetime relationship. Maybe it was inevitable that we would be drawn to each other within the particular confines of our circumstantial meeting. To find someone in Texas who actually liked labor unions was a rarity. But we each in our own way never quite fit into some conventional social norm that governed politics and policy in the great state of Texas.

In May John gave me an engagement ring for my twentieth birthday, and in June I gave him a senior ring for his college graduation. By October we were married.

Outsiders Together

John resumed his old full-time job as copy editor on the early morning desk of the *San Antonio Light*, the only Hearst newspaper in Texas at the time as well as the only fully unionized paper in our virulently anti-union state. Booze-loving sportswriters, aspiring novelists, and sardonic editors like John were very much in vogue in the still-booming newspaper industry in the 1960s. At the *Light* they were proud members of the left-leaning American Newspaper Guild, and John was its local president.[4] Our friends were drama critics, writers, art curators, politicians, and plumbers. Our weekends revolved around John's newspaper cronies. As a result, my eager start in adult life was living vicariously through John's daily engagement in the wider world. It was about all I could manage, because our children came so swiftly—two smart, beautiful, adorable, and demanding babies.

We lived on the upper level of a two-story duplex, with rented furniture and my Joan Miró print from college hanging over a makeshift bookshelf of boards supported by cement blocks. John's sister took pity on us: I carried laundry up and down stairs to a laundromat a few blocks away, and she paid for a diaper service for us. I was so busy tending to my babies that I was shocked years later to learn that I had never recognized the absolute seriousness of the Cuban Missile Crisis or other world events during that period. Of course, I kept up with the general news, and I knew this was something different, but I was totally dependent on John for my contacts with the outside world—both social and political.

John would call me almost every day to read a hot news item that had just appeared on the wire. Minutes after John F. Kennedy had been shot in Dallas, it was John who let me know. Only the day before, we had watched Kennedy's motorcade move through San Antonio. I saw the unfolding drama on television that fateful weekend, mostly alone with our one- and two-year-old toddlers. John camped out in the newsroom to stay on top of breaking news. But we were together on Sunday morning and watched Jack Ruby shoot Lee Harvey Oswald in front of a worldwide television audience. Life's highs and lows and the way they played out in news and politics were part of our marriage from the beginning. As shaken as we were after the assassination, the nation moved on. So did we.

El Extremo

John's first political nickname was "El Extremo." It would not be his last. Lean, tall, and ruddy with a few blond remnants of the tow-headed kid he had been, John carried a birdlike intensity in his blue eyes. That intensity and his hunched-up shoulders from a childhood of asthma-labored breathing made you think that he could pounce in anger at any moment. He didn't suffer fools and could be abrupt in cutting short a boring conversation or a meandering meeting. But I had seen the softness and vulnerability under that fierce intensity, and I loved the combination as well as the quickness of his mind. He knew what it was like to be an outsider, to be ignored as a sickly kid while life went on around him. I guess that matched with my own sense of being out of the mainstream because of my Sicilian name. We were a weird pair all right, surprisingly comfortable in our role as outsiders.

Although raised in the affluent Alamo Heights suburb of San Antonio, John immersed himself in union activities at the newspaper. He also got involved with the political work of the local central labor council. There he linked the writers and reporters of the *Light* with the brewery workers, plumbers, bus drivers, and telephone company linemen who were also helping organize San Antonio's low-wage Mexican American workers in a dozen different factories.

When the free-flowing cultural changes began to emerge in the mid-1960s, we did not drop out or drug out, although both of us had our flirtatious moments with the counterculture. Instead we got caught up in the politics of San Antonio's emerging Mexican American majority. We took part in union organizing, election-day block walks, and precinct phone banks. We labored in political campaigns for local candidates who were trying to bust up the age-old white business establishment that had long dominated San Antonio politics.

John was drawn to the raucous political moves of the dominant Mexican American politician, Albert Peña, who had headed the Viva Kennedy organizations in the 1960 presidential election. Surprisingly, Peña had gotten himself elected county commissioner to represent San Antonio's largely Mexican American West Side. It was the poorest area of the city, where urban slums rivaled the worst in the nation.

San Antonio schools were still racially segregated in the 1960s and reflected the cultural, racial, and economic divisions of the city itself, split almost evenly into four geographic quadrants. The affluent North Side was for middle-class and professional Anglos; the East Side was for African Americans; the South Side was an amalgamation of Polish and German working-class families and low-level civil service workers at Kelly Field, one of five major military bases in the area. And the West Side was almost exclusively for Mexican Americans. You could be born, live, and die on your side of town and never enter the other areas. Many people did just that. Most Anglos never ventured to the West Side, and many Mexican Americans never left the West Side, where Spanish was the dominant language.

Albert Peña believed he could change San Antonio, end segregation and discrimination, and alleviate poverty by leading a political movement to challenge the old San Antonio families whose cattle, cotton, and oil fortunes had allowed them to control every aspect of public life in the city.[5] His vision was to create a political base strong enough to challenge the North Side bankers and lawyers who ran city government as if it was their own private business. He began to pull together other dissident elements in the city—labor organizations, African Americans, poorly paid teachers, South Side working folks, and the few hundred well-to-do North Side liberals who were also shut out of power. With their support, he was able to create the Bexar County Democratic Coalition.[6] Because he had led the Latino effort to elect the Kennedy-Johnson ticket in 1960, Peña was able to hook into the Kennedy clan's political influence and money. Later he held sway over the local implementation of many of the Johnson-era Great Society programs on the West Side, where city services had been seriously neglected in comparison to other areas of the city. Peña's influence extended beyond San Antonio with his statewide leadership role in PASSO (Political Association of Spanish-Speaking Organizations), an outgrowth of the Viva Kennedy clubs. He was also a leader in a statewide coalition of liberal, labor, and minority organizations that formed a new organization—Democrats of Texas (DOT)—to wrest the state Democratic Party apparatus from the conservative faction that maintained a firm grip on political power in Texas.

In his free time after work, John began to write speeches for Peña and plot strategies with cronies called The Hook, The Fox, and other characters so aptly tagged in San Antonio's evolving and colorful West

With John Rogers and our young children, Billy (right) and Eleanor (left).

Side politics. Under the tutorship of Peña, John developed a knack for strategy and for articulating bold ideas that sprang so surprisingly from his quiet demeanor. Within the Democratic Coalition that was emerging in San Antonio, John quickly became "El Extremo." By default, in my early twenties I became "Mrs. Extremo." Yet we were primarily idealists rather than any kind of extremist agitators. Also, we were still enamored in one form or another with our chosen fields of journalism and writing.

We had the rather romantic dream of running our own community newspaper. Albert Peña encouraged us and gave us a corner of his law office to set up shop. We envisioned producing one of those free throwaway publications that would cover West Side news as well as political happenings in the city. However, neither of us knew anything about starting a newspaper from scratch or creating a business plan and marketing strategy to generate advertising. Our ill-fated venture produced only one issue and lasted no more than a month. But we were learning about the real world of politics, news, and life. For me, however, reality was back home with my toddlers.

My Time

By the time Eleanor and Billy were two and three years old, I had started volunteering for various political campaigns. My first effort was to help young lawyer Jim Barlow get elected district attorney. It was a minimal involvement, of course. I merely kept precinct files on my dining room table and made get-out-the-vote calls when the kids napped. Through that effort, I met other active Democrats, including retired noncommissioned military officer Hank Appel, who encouraged me to help him organize a club for North Side Democrats. Appel was one of those "numbers guys" who manually organized long lists of vote tallies by precinct lines. His meticulous precomputer algorithm targeting information guided many campaign efforts for Democratic Coalition–supported candidates. Because of these ventures, I was able to become friends with brilliant lawyer Herschel (Herky) Bernard, who was the brains and chief fundraiser behind most of the successful efforts to transform San Antonio. Herky and his wife, Loretta, were the social glue that held the disparate elements of the coalition together, with parties and soirees in their contemporary book-filled North Side home. Thanks to John's mother, Lib, who willingly took on babysitting duties for our young children, I was able to go to the parties, campaign events, precinct organizing meetings, and sprawling rallies. We were also able to have a vibrant social life that opened a whole new world for me.

John and I sometimes hung out at the home of writers Hart and Annie Stilwell, who hosted small Friday night gatherings with writers and politicians. They always had a big pot of chili and plenty of booze waiting. Maury Maverick Jr. and his artist wife, Julia, were regulars on those evenings. Maury had been one of a small group of liberal hell-raisers who served in the state legislature in the 1950s. After his legislative service, Maury took up his law practice in San Antonio, where he was a pro bono American Civil Liberties Union attorney who defended civil rights protesters, atheists, Communists, and conscientious objectors trying to avoid the Vietnam-era military draft.

Maverick came by it all naturally. His father, Maury Maverick Sr., had been a favorite of FDR and staunch supporter of the New Deal while a member of Congress. Later he was probably the most controversial mayor who ever served in San Antonio because he supported free speech for Communists and other dissidents and allowed them to hold marches through the streets of the city. Maury Sr. also coined the term "gobbledygook" for unintelligible, bureaucratic double-speak. I was in awe of fierce intellectual champions like the legendary Mavericks, who were so actively engaged in San Antonio's life and culture.

As I began to know more people who were politically active, I had opportunities to hone my political skills by working on voter registration drives on the West Side. Albert Peña was making a major effort to register Latino voters. Federal courts had not yet struck down the state's onerous "poll tax," so Texans had to come up with money to purchase the right to vote.[7] I will never forget my experience of going into a West Side meatpacking plant to sell poll taxes to Mexican American and African American workers, who were still wearing their blood-stained white aprons while they folded out their crumpled dollars to buy the right to vote. I was shocked and determined to do more to bring about change in these barriers to voting.

When Cesar Chavez later began an organizing drive among migrant farmworkers in South Texas, I was one of those Anglo housewives who helped organize grocery store boycotts of Texas melons and California grapes that came from anti-union farm conglomerates. John and I marched in San Antonio and Austin with the farmworkers as they made the trek from the Rio Grande Valley to the state capital to push for a $1.25/hour minimum wage for those who labored in the fields. Through our minimal activities supporting the fledgling United Farm Workers union, I got to know a group of young Mexican American college students and activists like Willie Velasquez, Ernesto Cortes, and Rosie Castro. All would later make their marks in the world: Velasquez would establish the Southwest Voter Education Project to register Mexican American voters; Cortes would receive a MacArthur "genius grant" for his effective community organizing efforts throughout the Southwest; and Castro would become a leader in the new La Raza Unida political party and the mother of charismatic twins: Julián Castro, who served as mayor of San Antonio and was a presidential candidate in 2020, and Joaquin Castro, who serves in the US Congress.

As soon as our kids could walk and talk, John and I took them to union meetings and farmworker rallies, and they slept on my lap at political gatherings until they were old enough to hand out leaflets or carry signs. Our social life, our identity, and later even our livelihood began to center more and more around the political world. Soon I started getting offers to work for pay in short-term political campaigns. I loved every minute of these mini-adventures, even though they put an enormous strain on my child-rearing efforts. However, my campaign work provided us with a little extra money on a seasonal basis.

With our newfound savings and the help of my parents, we were able to put a down payment on a small home in the Alamo Heights School District, where John had been educated. By the time our children entered elementary school, I had managed to go back to the University of Texas to finish my degree, interrupted earlier by my marriage and pregnancies. With the kids in school, I had time to do more.

Mrs. Extremo's Awakening

The 1960s were a time of enormous change in San Antonio as well as the nation. John wrote articles for the independent and influential *Texas Observer* and other publications. He took a look at the increasing political influence of the burgeoning Mexican American population, an awakening "sleeping giant" that seemed always to be on the verge of becoming a factor in electoral politics in San Antonio but not quite making it. He wrote pieces about the union-busting efforts of some of Texas's largest employers and deepened his role in union organizing in San Antonio.

I also started writing occasionally for the *Observer*. I was fascinated by the left-leaning Catholic priests who saw the Second Vatican Council in Rome as a call to arms for social justice for their Mexican American parishioners and I followed their activities for the *Observer*. I once raised the ire of the San Antonio business community by writing about how business owners secretly got the city government to use its power of eminent domain to decimate whole Mexicano and African American neighborhoods on the edge of downtown to obtain enough land to build "Hemisfair '68," a mini–world's fair that they hoped would bring new business to the city. My first brush with public criticism brought a mix of pride and fear. I was proud because the article touched a nerve and brought to light a common but secretive practice in the city. Yet I was uncomfortable with the recognition that the article brought me. Why had I so carelessly made myself known and become a target of powerful people? My Sicilian fears continued to undermine my public confidence and would remain a source of anxiety over the years.

My own growing activism in San Antonio politics was also a time of discovery of Mexican history and art, enhanced after John and I took several trips into interior Mexico. Local Mexican American culture fascinated me as well. I loved the *conjunto* accordion music at political rallies. I loved the bold colors and the inexpensive "folk art" that I began to collect in San Antonio's small shops as well as the downtown Mexican market. I loved Albert Peña's fiery speeches and call to arms, and I admired his then-wife Olga's toughness when facing obstacles in a campaign. I loved the way whole families attended the neighborhood rallies together, with young children and old grandparents in tow. My increasing connections with an appealing Mexican culture were the beginning of my rediscovery of the values of the Sicilian upbringing that I had largely ignored once I left home to go to college.

I remember vividly the night it came back to me. We were at a West Side political rally at Mission Park. As the music played, an old grandfather asked his little granddaughter to dance with him. I watched as they held hands and danced a polka across the floor. Tears inexplicably came to my eyes. The sight of the little girl's delight touched something deep within me. I remembered being thrilled to get to dance with my dad or my uncles at those big Sicilian weddings attended by three or four generations of the same families. I realized that Mexican American Catholic family-oriented people exerted a pull on me because of my own experiences in a similar culture.

I admit that I had a romantic view of politics at the time. I saw only the hopeful glittering reflection of sunlight on our actions. Fighting with others in social justice causes seemed to be both noble and dangerously exciting. I was thrilled to be included when members of Albert Peña's Democratic Coalition began meeting every Friday for lunch in the private room of a popular West Side Mexican restaurant. I loved the conversations about the week's events and its heroes and villains. I was rarely a participant in those discussions, more often a silent lurker happy to be in the room where lots of "big" talk occurred and serious people made serious plans to change San Antonio. But changing the political culture in San Antonio would not be easy.

The Black Hand over San Antonio

Reality began to set in with the 1966 Democratic primary elections, in which John and I were both deeply involved. We thought the coalition's West Side neighborhoods plus labor unions, teachers, African Americans, and North Side liberals were on the verge of taking power by electing a majority of members of the Bexar County Commissioner's Court, which was the five-member body that controlled the city's major charity hospital, public works, tax collection, and myriad other important functions. It was there that our friend Albert Peña had broken the race barrier to enter San Antonio politics. Now he was mounting a major campaign to elect a popular Latino attorney to the group that also included the coalition-backed county judge Charles Grace, who was the presiding officer of the body and highest elected official in the county.

Almost half of San Antonio's 235,000 registered voters lived in city and county precincts where the coalition candidates had shown strength in previous elections. This was to be the time when power in the city would finally shift away from the wealthy Anglo families that had dominated its local politics for over a century. But a television commercial in the final days of the campaign changed everything. It began with a huge Black Hand hovering menacingly over the skyline of San Antonio. An ominous voice boomed its message: "Militant minorities of our city are making a grandstand play to take over Bexar County." In the key visual frame, political leader Peña was seen whispering into the ear of the court's presiding officer, Charles Grace, who was puffing on a huge cigar. The implication was clear. Mexican Peña called the shots: Grace was nothing more than a puppet. Add one more Latino to the mix and there would be a radical Mexican takeover. The same photograph in the TV ad was printed on 100,000 flyers mailed to voters in Anglo-dominated precincts.

We laughed about the ad. Who would believe that Mexican hordes would take over and destroy the city? Or that Peña represented the forces of evil depicted in the ads? Of course, that was because we were trapped in our delusional belief that rational voters could not possibly be persuaded by campaign rhetoric built on fear and racism. But the majority of San Antonio voters obviously feared that the city was on the verge of a radical racial change, which they did not want. By a two-to-one margin, they threw Grace out of office and managed to defeat almost every coalition-supported candidate on the ballot. With the 1966 election, the local bankers, lawyers, and old society family members had used their money and moxie to keep the growing Mexican American population from coming to power in the city. It would happen again and again.

It took me a long time to learn the true lesson of the Black Hand campaign. Against all evidence to the contrary, I simply could not understand how voters could so easily be deceived or how outright lies and overt racism could prevail against "truth and justice." I continued to hold on to the belief that this particular election loss was somehow a fluke. It took many more years of election losses for the reality of fear-based campaign victories to break apart my optimistic illusions.

By the time of the Black Hand election, I had been involved in minor roles in many campaigns—from working in local offices for statewide candidates to helping elect candidates to the San Antonio City Council. We won some. We lost some. But I was lucky enough to take a break from the incessant turmoil of political campaigns when I was offered a job with a quasi-federal agency that focused its efforts on improving living conditions on the West Side.

With Billy and Eleanor in school, I felt that I would have the time to take on a full-time professional job in the Model Cities Program, where I wrote federal grant proposals for school lunch and breakfast programs for poor schools in the area. My first boss was young Henry Cisneros, later to become the first Hispanic mayor of San Antonio and a member of President Bill Clinton's cabinet. But even before I had fully settled into my new job, John and I were also facing some major changes in how we lived our lives.

John had always been more realistic about politics than I was, and he understood that fundamental change in San Antonio would not happen quickly. He had begun spending more time in Austin, where his part-time work for the state labor federation allowed him to be involved in statewide politics and leave the political wars in San Antonio behind. He was beginning to sharpen his organizational and political skills, and his position as an editor on the *Light*'s copy desk was boring by comparison. He finally left the newspaper world in 1969 to take a higher-paying, full-time job in Austin with the Texas AFL-CIO.

John's opportunity for a deeper political role within the Texas labor movement created a major dilemma for me. The school year had already started. Six-year-old Eleanor had entered the first grade only weeks earlier and Billy was now in the third grade. I didn't want to disrupt their bright beginnings. Besides, I was beginning to love my new job in the Model Cities Program. I felt that I was finally coming into my own in San Antonio with a rich social and professional life and was deeply torn about the possibility of leaving it behind. Ultimately, I decided to remain with our children in San Antonio. John would make the effort to drive back to San Antonio from Austin each weekend to be with us.

Some of our friends thought we had a sophisticated arrangement with our separate lives in different cities. But after a few months, it didn't feel sophisticated. It felt confusing. My life was less balanced without John. I was on the go constantly, juggling my work, politics, and our household on my own. I was unsettled and fitful. But San Antonio politics was unsettling as well.

After the Black Hand election, our Friday coalition luncheons were becoming a little less collegial and moved to a smaller venue owned by one of the younger Chicano activists. Many of the younger college students Albert Peña had brought into local politics were acutely aware that the often-inept strategies of the older leaders were not working. They wanted less talk and more action, and many were attracted to the fledgling separatist La Raza Unida Party that had gained a foothold in Crystal City, southwest of San Antonio. Although I was still in my twenties and close in age to most of these students, I was often uncomfortable with the more militant rhetoric. But the times *were* troubling and called for significant change, given what was going on across the country with growing anti–Vietnam war protests and the realities of Richard Nixon's first term in office. I began to take part in peace vigils on Sunday nights in front of the Alamo and served on the board of the local ACLU, where Maury Maverick Jr. was handling dozens of conscientious-objector cases. But I also had an emerging practical side that began to push away some of my romantic attachment to San Antonio's increasingly volatile politics. Perhaps a glimmer of Sicilian skepticism began to allow me to see the futility of the direction some coalition members were taking. Whatever we were doing was not working.

By late spring in 1970 I was ready to leave San Antonio to join John in Austin. He also felt the strain of our commuter marriage and wanted us to be together again. When the school year ended, we took a long East Coast vacation with the children and came back to Texas to settle into an idyllic little duplex along Waller Creek in Austin, just north of the University of Texas campus. It would be another ten years before San Antonio would really begin to change, and we missed the transformation that we had hoped to achieve in our youth. Although the efforts of the Democratic Coalition might have laid a foundation for the change, albeit rather shaky, it played only a secondary role in San Antonio's eventual transformation, which was led by one of the young men Albert Peña had mentored and encouraged to learn and lead. By the late 1970s Ernesto Cortes, community organizer extraordinaire, had created a grassroots tsunami of West Side neighborhood and parish organizations whose actions would change San Antonio forever.

Although my San Antonio experiences always remained deep in my heart, Austin would become my home for the next three decades. There John would come into his own as a hard-edged strategist and make his mark on Texas politics—not as "El Extremo" but as "Nuke." In Austin the illusionary romance of politics for me began to give way to a reality and reluctant practicality that proved far more challenging. My days as "Mrs. Extremo" would be numbered.

PART III

It's a Texas Thing

Austin

One Sunday afternoon shortly after we moved to Austin, John and I took our children to the twentieth wedding anniversary party of Ann and David Richards. The state's progressive glitterati filled their West Lake Hills home and spilled out into the backyard that overlooked the Austin skyline. The children had garlands of flowers in their hair, and activities were organized for their amusement. The gathering could have been a glamorous photo-shoot for a Town & Country *magazine spread.*

I was enchanted, of course, and considered myself lucky to be included in such a clever group of Texas's liberal and progressive elites.

It was not as it seemed. Nor was Austin.

WHEN WE MOVED TO AUSTIN as a family in the summer of 1970, we lived on the banks of Waller Creek in a charming little duplex just north of the University of Texas campus. Our children could play in the creek, which was washed clean every evening when the old swimming pool at nearby Shipe Park was emptied, because it had no modern filtration system. Who knows what really flowed down that creek, but it seemed so ideally Austin, with its oak trees and rock outcroppings, and reminded us of our student days. Billy and Eleanor settled into the small inner-city Lee Elementary School, which was surprisingly diverse for the time.[1]

We were happy to be together in our Waller Creek home, and later we got to live in other wonderful neighborhoods with backyards full of squirrels and oak trees and our old dog Spot. We enjoyed our weekend boat rides on Texas Hill Country lakes, occasionally anchoring in a peaceful cove to swim or picnic. Austin was a wonderful place to raise our children, watch them grow up, and have opportunities for college and interesting lives.

Still, it was politics that first attracted and pulled us full force into Austin life.

At the time, the remnants of the ultraconservative John Connally crowd were running all things political in Texas, including Austin's local government. Smart, arrogant, and imperious, John Connally had been the dominant presence in Democratic state politics for over a decade and had just finished his third term as Texas governor.

Texas liberals and labor leaders had numerous reasons to hate Connally: his financial ties to the oil industry, his anti-union posturing and slightly veiled racism, and his deep enmity toward liberal hero Ralph Yarborough during their recurring struggles to control the state's Democratic Party. But what particularly rankled John and me was his disrespect for upcoming Latino leaders. He once demanded that a photograph of our friend Bexar county commissioner Albert Peña be removed from an exhibit at the Institute of Texan Cultures that highlighted the contributions of Mexican Americans to the state. When he brought the heavily armed Texas Rangers with him to stare down the ragtag bunch of Rio Grande Valley farmworkers on their long highway march to the capital to secure a $1.25/hour minimum wage for field hands, he became a permanent fixture in the liberal pantheon of villains. But Connally's former aides were still in charge of most governmental functions throughout the state in the early 1970s, and the oft-hapless liberals had not yet figured out a strategy to dislodge them.

John and I were like a lot of graduates of the University of Texas, for whom Austin was always a magical city. Although John had returned before I did, I was still eager to participate in the Austin liberal scene. The capital city had always had its leftist cabals made up of dissident writers, lawyers, college professors, state employees, and radical students drawn to politics, booze, and country music. They usually gathered to rant and rave late afternoons at Scholz Garten, an old German beer joint just south of the university campus. I loved the stories of their adventures, usually embellished in the *Texas Observer*, the progressive statewide newspaper that allowed Texas liberals to feel part of some cohesive holy cause, even though they were almost always shut out of positions of power. The *Observer* was in its heyday in the 1970s, with fiery populist editors Jim Hightower, Kaye Northcott, and the quick-witted satirist Molly Ivins, who could make readers laugh and cry at the same time when she reported the absurdities that spewed out of the Texas legislature on a regular basis.

We hit Austin at the beginning of the famous Armadillo World Headquarters, the old armory that creative entrepreneur Eddie Wilson had converted to a music hall. The Armadillo's developing progressive, country-rock music scene was enhanced and romanticized when Willie Nelson moved to Austin from Nashville and became a regular there. Performers like Janis Joplin, Bette Midler, Ray Charles, Leon Russell, Stevie Ray Vaughan, Freddie King, Frank Zappa, ZZ Top, Jerry Jeff Walker, and dozens of other renowned musicians wowed the locals. Austin became the go-to place for musicians on the make. Their wilder fans followed. The so-called weirdness that Austin prizes today actually started with the old Armadillo, which was named for the scruffy, ugly, hard-shelled nocturnal animal that has no natural predators and is ubiquitous in the Hill Country. The Armadillo art of poster artist extraordinaire Jim Franklin conveyed a visual attitude that thumbed its nose at Austin's conservative elite and captured the new outlaw culture, as if to say: "We too are ubiquitous. We're free to do what we want and we don't give a damn what you think." Austin would soon bill itself as the "live-music capital of the world." A vibrant counterculture was emerging that would give Austin the "cool" vibe that it struggles to hold on to today. While Austin was becoming culturally cool, however, staid old bankers and lawyers who were disdainful of the growing hoard of hippies who flocked to the city still controlled its politics. Austin had a veneer of collegiality, but the political climate was dysfunctional. The old guard was unprepared for the challenges to come.

New Opportunities

While John solidified his role as the communications director and later as political director for the state AFL-CIO federation, I enrolled in the graduate School of Architecture, hoping to get my master's degree in urban planning. But I was quickly bored. After working for a year in the federal Model Cities program on the West Side of San Antonio, I was more interested in practical solutions to transform cities than were some of my professors, whose minds were wrapped up in the humane design elements of the New Town movements represented by Reston, Virginia, and Columbia, Maryland. While all of that was important to improve the quality of urban life, I was missing the excitement of the raucous politics and power struggles in San Antonio. After only one semester, I wanted to plunge back into a more political world.

Danny Ruiz, a rising Latino leader, offered me a job in the Austin Model Cities Program, somewhat similar to my work in San Antonio. But I wanted something different. For me, difference came in the form of Bob Armstrong, a charming young legislator from Austin who had just won statewide election for land commissioner, whose job was to oversee 22 million acres of state-owned land and Texas coastal waters. In his campaign, Armstrong had talked about land-use planning and sound environmental policies for the whole state of Texas, a radical thought here in the 1970s. His message was appealing to me, and I thought it would be interesting to be involved in a new adventure to bring about significant change on a much larger scale.

Rangy, blunt-talking Hank Brown, who was the visionary president of the Texas AFL-CIO and John's boss, called Armstrong on my behalf. I became a political "must-hire," one of those people elected officials hire as a favor to someone who is powerful. Because Armstrong had not yet hired a press secretary, I simply slipped into that role. I wrote lots of press releases, edited agency reports, and even co-wrote a beauti- fully illustrated history of Texas public lands.[2] But that was not enough to keep me busy, so I started searching for other things to do in the agency. I surprised myself by discovering that the administration and management of a 200-employee state agency could be quite fascinating. Bob, who was extraordinarily kind and good-natured, encouraged me to venture out and take on an executive-level role to develop personnel policies and grievance procedures as well as to help shape his legislative agenda. Most importantly for my learning curve, I began to help coor- dinate the budgeting process and write the narratives that justified our spending requests. Because the budget had to be approved by the Texas legislature, I also got to dip my toes into state-house politics. And what about land-use planning and environmental safeguards?

As it turned out, the land commissioner had very little authority in the area. His main duties were to administer, audit, and collect royalties from oil and gas leases on state-owned lands, supervise Texas beaches and coastal waters, and run a low-cost loan program to help military veterans buy rural land. Only later when a federal Coastal Land Management Program was authorized during the Nixon administration did the Land Office gain authority and money to plan and develop regulations for wetlands protection along the Texas Gulf Coast. By this time, I had taken on so many other duties that I could only grimace when Bob brought in a high-paid consulting group to manage the new coastal planning program. They tended to ignore the marine biologists and environmentalists we already had on our staff. The consultants represented everything I came to dislike about government outsourcing: an arrogant supremacy of expertise that was dismissive of local experience and basic common sense. The antidote to the enshrinement of this kind of expertise led me right back to the grassroots politics that I had come to love—one more time.

The Heady Heat of Star Power

For many women in the early 1970s, the best way to be deeply involved in Texas politics was through some man. Few women today in politics would have to make that admission. Yet, at the time, I felt lucky to be tangentially involved in organized labor's projects through John's increasing political activism. Now, however, I was also working professionally for a shining star on the Texas political scene. Through Bob Armstrong's connections, I had the opportunity to learn what was really happening at the center of Texas politics. Yet, as charming as he could be, Bob was a loner of sorts among the dominant political factions at play in Austin. While he had strong social ties with key members of the conservative Democratic Party establishment through

Bob Armstrong was elected land commissioner in 1970, after serving in the Texas legislature. I served as his press aide for five years. He later served as assistant secretary for land and minerals management at the US Department of the Interior. He returned to Austin, where we worked together again during Governor Ann Richards's administration. We remained lifelong friends.

his family, he was steadily becoming more liberal and was the hero of the Scholz Garten political groupies.

Bob seemed to revel in the attention of the fun-loving liberals. He was witty and clever and could pull out his guitar, strum, and sing when the occasion demanded. A man of many talents, he continuously sought new experiences in everything from flying his own airplane to buying bull semen for his Red Brangus cows. He hunted deer with a bow and arrow, organized raft trips on the rapids of the Rio Grande, and created a chili con queso dip that still bears his name in restaurants from Austin to Washington, DC. Bob would spend months planning an annual weekend campout at his ranch outside of Austin that drew liberals, lawyers, journalists, and assorted activists from all over the state. Sometimes they got a little wild late at night as the booze kicked in and the kids were safely tucked away and sleeping in their tents. But it was not just the campouts that reflected the good times among the liberal community in Austin. A new sense of freedom was emerging, and the margins were being pushed everywhere.

While I was working for Bob, it was often beer and Mexican food at lunch, wine or whiskey in the late afternoon, and a round of receptions after dark. Because he was such a handsome good-timer and loved honky-tonk dancing at the Broken Spoke, Bob was a magnet for Austin's fun-loving party girls, some of whom he liked and others he avoided. Although I was occasionally invited along, I was never a part of Bob's nighttime prowls. My young children were at home; they needed dinner and help with their homework. John was often away in the evenings because of some labor or legislative intrigue, so I just wanted to go home after work to be with my kids.

It was also increasingly important to me at the time that Bob trusted me to keep an eye on the agency. I couldn't really keep tabs on the bureaucratic mischief and turf battles in the office if I went out for two-hour lunches, indulged in nightly bar tours, or traipsed around in the woods following Bob and the deer hunters. I became a drag and a drudge yet was always kindly tolerated by my party-loving boss.

Although I rarely joined the Scholz crowd or its more intellectual and wilder counterpart—the Raw Deal, where Ann and David Richards were hanging out—I was still in the grips of politics. With the anti-war movement in full force and my horror at the Vietnam conflict growing daily, I could not resist plunging into the early stages of the 1972 George McGovern presidential campaign. Austin's liberal community loved the free-for-all endless debates and drama in Democratic Party politics. I let myself be absorbed into meeting after meeting, hearing the same arguments over and over. Practicality aside, it was still fun to be on the floor at a rowdy state political party convention. I was proud when my young children wore their McGovern T-shirts. But after the national conventions, when the Nixon reelection campaign really heated up, reality settled in for me.

Bob Armstrong was the chair of the McGovern presidential effort in Texas, and his main job was to oversee two darling, totally inexperienced young men that the McGovern campaign sent to run the operation. One was Taylor Branch, who would become the Pulitzer

Prize–winning biographer of Martin Luther King Jr. The other was a guy named Bill Clinton, who brought along his girlfriend, Hillary Rodham. Bob had such a great time traveling around the state with them that he did not seem to see the inevitability of Nixon's victory. Even as inexperienced as I was at the time about the nature of statewide campaigns, I could see that the general election efforts were disastrous. I was not sure I wanted any part of it and buried myself in General Land Office work.

After that election, my excitement about politics would be scaled down and become much more practical.

Perhaps I was beginning to come to grips with the reality of my own maturity, which psychologists believe provides the opportunity to fully integrate our personality with the larger purpose in our lives. I now realize that I was struggling to do just that during the decade of my thirties. I began to question everything.

Inner Detour

I had taken on too many responsibilities at work and spent most of my time dodging employee turf battles, as well as dealing with all of the normal hassles of entrenched bureaucracies. My desire for perfection both in the office and at home aroused an anxiety that was making me increasingly uncomfortable. I even thought I might be developing an ulcer. I found a weekly meditation class that I thought could help me relax, and it just happened to be in the offices of Austin's Jung Society. But it was the Jung Society's fabulous bookstore that was more alluring than meditation.

I began reading more about philosophy and psychology, particularly Carl Jung and his followers like the Italian writer Roberto Assagioli, one of the pioneers in the humanistic psychology movement. Like Jung, Assagioli stressed the spiritual dimension in the process of personal self-awareness and transformation. This appealed to me. Perhaps all of those Catholic Masses with my father's family and Methodist sermons in my mother's church made me susceptible to some other dimension

in life. As busy as I was in those early years in Austin, I was probably unconsciously looking for some deeper stage of self-awareness to
cope more effectively with my evolving professional and family life. I
wanted to be connected to something larger and deeper than my own
ego and the daily grind of life. Yet the writings of Jungian-influenced
thinkers provoked more questions about my role in life than answers.

Was I primarily the mother of young children? A helpmate to my
busy husband? An advocate for worthy causes? A political operative or
a budding administrator? Could I face the truth that I was an aspiring
writer who never took the time to write? Who was I actually destined
to be? Or was the notion of destiny itself a fraud and another illusion?
As Thomas Merton has written, "We are not very good at recognizing
illusions, least of all the ones we cherish about ourselves."³ I think all of
this was at the core of my deeper questioning: who the hell was I? My
inherent restlessness, plus this inner confusion over my essential role in
the world, inevitably led to even more inner conflict and anxiety that
was hard to shake.

I was looking for some sort of inner serenity that I could not find
in either the religious platitudes of my Methodist youth or the self-
help aphorisms of my young adulthood. I started keeping a journal
at the time, mainly to figure out what I was thinking and feeling that
was so internally challenging. Now I understand that I was beginning
some sort of spiritual search that was enormously compelling as well as
terribly confusing. Some of my new readings, particularly those of the
Vietnamese Buddhist monk Thich Nhat Hanh, offered inner medita-
tions and mantras designed to help let go of fear, ponder deeper issues,
and become more self-aware in a quest to achieve some sort of personal
balance. When I came across those old secret journals years later, it
was obvious that I was feeling a need for some heartfelt experiences of
meaning—hinted at but not completely manifest in my political world.

But my political world was changing at the time. It seemed to be
bristling with new opportunities for women like me, and I was loath
to abandon it for some inchoate spiritual search that only seemed to
add to my confusion and inner conflict. As Thomas Merton once said,
"before you have a spiritual life, you've got to have a life."⁴ And I still

very much wanted to have a political life. I gradually moved out of Bob Armstrong's political orbit and wanted to develop something on my own, even though I was not sure exactly what it might be.

The People's Republic of Austin

At home, politics in Austin was becoming as compelling for me as San Antonio politics had been only a few years earlier. After a lawsuit allowing University of Texas students to vote in Austin elections, a wave of 25,000 new young voters helped wrest the city council away from the bankers, lawyers, and old Connally crowd that controlled the city. Austin was evolving. Power was shifting.

I jumped into city politics to help elect my friend Dr. Emma Lou Linn to the city council. Austin was on the verge of its first major growth spurt, and the rapid expansion promoted by aggressive real-estate developers was becoming a threat to the quality of the underground aquifer and Austin's glorious spring-fed Barton Springs pool as well as the pristine blue hills that the developers wanted to chop up into subdivisions. Dr. Linn, who was a professor of psychology at St. Edward's University, and other progressives on the city council struggled to put reasonable restrictions on the new growth. She was a champion of fledgling preservation efforts to save the wonderful old Victorian homes on the edge of Austin's downtown area. At her urging, I served on a historical preservation committee, but we were powerless to save most of the old structures. Everything in the city was changing, and the ascendancy of new liberal leadership was soon overwhelmed by the dynamics of a fundamental shift to a booming economy.

The high-tech revolution was in its early stages in the 1980s when Austin landed the Microelectronics and Computer Technology Research Consortium (MCC), the nation's first and largest computer industry research and development organization. Almost everything in the city began to change after MCC. Under the direction of Admiral Bobby Ray Inman, who had been head of the National Security

Agency, MCC focused on artificial intelligence, hardware and software design, information management, and network design. The consortium spawned dozens of new technology companies in Austin. In 1984 Michael Dell launched his computer business that generated thousands of new jobs and tremendous new wealth for its original employee stockholders, whose stock soon exceeded millions of dollars in value. The "Dellionaires" would ultimately change the nature of business and philanthropy in Austin. Fortunately, their politics were generally progressive, but they aggressively pursued new ventures that expanded the business culture of the city. Austin was quickly shifting away from its days as the relaxed, idyllic Hill Country mecca that housed the state's flagship university and the seat of Texas government. It was becoming more—or less, depending on your point of view.

By 1980 even the Armadillo World Headquarters had been razed to put up another office building. Perhaps there is no greater symbol of what was happening in Austin than the story of the little local hippie grocery store on North Lamar. Whole Foods Market, which specialized in organic produce, was becoming so successful that it quickly evolved into a modern corporate growth-oriented, market-driven national chain, eventually owned by Amazon.

During those years, my attention was more focused on the progressive shift in the city than on the changing business climate. I jumped at every opportunity to be involved in political campaigns and policy actions. I served as co-chair of an Austin charter revision commission as well as head of the city's first Ethics Commission. Neither was popular with the city's business establishment, though they were not nearly as effective as we had hoped they might be, often generating more controversy than consensus. The Charter Commission proposed so many radical and unrealistic changes for city government that its report was quickly ignored and forgotten. The newly formed Ethics Commission had no support from city staff, and its first case involved a conflict-of-interest charge against a developer who served on the city's Planning Commission. The public hearing was basically derailed by a former city attorney who represented the developer and undercut the process by forcing us into a quagmire of meaningless votes. While I still had some of the impulses of my old "Mrs. Extremo" days, I was learning that impulses had limits and could blind me to the reality of a situation. My public actions in various Austin political campaigns also meant that I was becoming "known." It was not always comfortable.

Although I no longer worked for Bob Armstrong, we remained friends, and I continued to help him whenever he asked. I even went with him on a fundraising call to meet with one of the richest and most powerful men in Austin, who had also recently served as the downtown business establishment's favorite mayor. As we entered the study in his palatial home, the former mayor handed me a copy of Chairman Mao's *Little Red Book*, a collection of 267 aphorisms from Chinese Communist leader Mao Zedong that was quite popular among radical students on American college campuses. With a sneer on his face, he said, "Mary Beth, I just want you to feel comfortable here." Of course, his intention was to make me as uncomfortable as possible. Yet, despite the economic power and assumed superiority of the establishment bigwigs who liked to pull rank over activist liberals, the city was slipping from their grasp politically. In fact, Austin was soon to be known as the People's Republic of Austin, the center of a new, aggressive antiestablishment politics in Texas, even as the real-estate developers and high-tech companies were gaining ascendancy and maneuvering to co-opt a smattering of liberal officeholders.

Political and Personal Shifts

With the 1975 extension of the Voting Rights Act to include Texas and Hispanics in the Southwest under its protection, the Texas legislature also began to change. Texas's most powerful business, banking, oil and gas interests, utilities, and insurance companies were facing serious challenges for the first time since the Great Depression. And serious Texas liberals slowly began to accumulate noticeable political clout.

When the political world began to offer such concrete new hope on so many new fronts—both local and statewide—I was even more hooked on political life than ever before. Yet I had also learned something about myself as I plunged even more deeply into the muddy well of Texas politics.

I had become a "generalist" in politics rather than a detailed policy specialist. Although I wanted to see definite policy changes enacted, I was usually satisfied to learn the broad brushstrokes and leave the details to others. I never felt the need to become one of those single-issue experts who had facts and numbers at their fingertips. Instead, I became enthralled with the broader elements of strategy and planning. What I most enjoyed was trying to figure out a path to implement policies that I thought merited our attention. I wanted to create an effective sequence of activities based on research, capacity, and realistic opportunities. I was learning how to look for patterns, and I loved to figure out the logistics of using them to our benefit. To operate at this level in politics, I had to change my frame of reference and move deeper, below the surface attractions in our passing political show. I began to ask a different set of questions about politics and policy. What has led to this particular dilemma? What connects it to something else more difficult to see? Who is saying what about the problem and what is their angle? Who has the power to block or initiate action? What is another way to look at this or that? The answers to all of those questions could be used to shape a political plan or strategy that just might lead to success.

I was also learning something else: maybe I was becoming more comfortable in taking a calculated risk to advance a cause or campaign venture. I was learning that sometimes you have to act before you have all the answers to your "deeper" questions. After all, in politics you could never predict with certainty what the outcome would be. That total unpredictability would be a hard lesson to learn. Yet by the time I had run both winning and losing statewide campaigns for Ann Richards in the 1990s, I had learned to shift my focus from hope about some eventual magical outcome in order to concentrate on whatever I could be doing each day to keep a well-conceived plan in action. I was learning to follow a plan while being flexible enough to adjust it when conditions warranted. For me, that was the only way to survive a loss or savor a victory in the muddy muck of Texas politics. Fundamentally, it meant that I was taking lessons from that inner world that were beginning to give me enough courage to plunge deeper into my life and work and avoid putting all my hopes into some idealized world that did not exist. Although I was still a liberal idealist in my beliefs, I was becoming much more practical in my actions. I wanted to win the struggles that engaged my imagination. And I was beginning to learn how.

Campaigns

The word "campaign" comes from campagne, *the French term for open, level country. It evolved from there into military vocabulary, where it was first used to denote the amount of time an army was kept in the field. Later it would be used to describe a particular military operation.*

Over time in Western democracies, the word came to refer to the process of getting elected to public office. But the idea that political campaigns are a form of combat still remains.

When Franklin Roosevelt accepted the Democratic Party nomination for president in the midst of the Great Depression, he told his followers, "This is more than a political campaign, it is a call to arms."[1]

It took a long time for Texas liberals like me to learn that effective campaigns are always a call to arms. If we wanted to win, we had to have better weapons, better reconnaissance of the terrain, and more strategic battle plans.

We also needed a whole lot of damn good luck.

MY VENTURE INTO DEEPER LEVELS of political activity was enhanced after John and I attended a political campaign workshop at Kent State University sponsored by the national AFL-CIO and Democratic Party operatives. We had the opportunity to sit at the feet of the godfather of the professional political consulting business: Matt Reese. Reese got his beginning in John F. Kennedy's presidential campaign in 1960 and worked for most of the national Democratic titans in the 1970s and 1980s. He was among the first to combine polling, demographic data, and computer techniques to identify specific clusters of voters for whom particular issues might have special meaning. It was from Reese, pollster Peter Hart, and others that we learned the basic mechanics of running political campaigns.

Reese was a big man in body and spirit—over six feet tall and almost three hundred pounds. I was in awe of the exuberant Reese as I sat in a small classroom and watched him lay out the basic key principle to follow in running political campaigns: *one-on-one repetitive contact between the candidate and the voter.* In the technology available at the time, repetitive contacts could be achieved in four different ways—media, mail, message, and personal interaction. Most importantly, they should be directed at specific targeted voters on whom all of your efforts should be concentrated. Reese taught us how to look for potential voters who were already in favor of our candidates and those who could be persuaded. "If you want to pick cherries, go where the cherries are," he told us.[2] This is a basic truism of political campaigns today, but the mechanics of selective targeting were not as sophisticated in the 1970s as they are now.

When I was still working for Bob Armstrong, I had also started reading the works of management guru Peter Drucker. From Drucker I learned to articulate what had always been intuitive for me: people do things for their own reasons, not yours. Or, in the world of political messaging, if you want to persuade voters to vote for your candidate, you have to give them a message that is personal and relevant to them. This is self-evident in most effective modern campaigns today, but it was an eye-opening revelation to me in the 1970s. When we fail to follow these simple guidelines—even today—we lose—again and again.

Ann Richards gave me the opportunity to put some of my new learning into practice. In 1976 Ann ran her first successful race for Travis County commissioner in West Austin. I jumped into her campaign wholeheartedly. We developed a game plan and "relevant" messages. I created mail pieces and produced TV spots for her. That effort cemented a personal and political relationship that would last for decades. After Ann's victory, I decided to leave my job with Bob Armstrong to set up a little consulting shop—mainly writing newsletters and developing brochures, political campaign materials, and grant proposals for nonprofit organizations, as well as helping women run for office. But I also had opportunities to be involved in statewide political efforts.

Branching Out

Shortly after we moved to Austin in 1970, I volunteered in the campaign for young Gonzalo Barrientos, who became the first Mexican American state representative from Austin and would go on to become a state senator and important leader in the growing progressive community in Texas. Because the 1965 Voting Rights Act and federal court orders had led to the creation of more minority-friendly legislative districts, Texas had its first generation of Latino and African American lawmakers since Reconstruction. The Reverend Zan Holmes, a brilliant African American minister from Dallas, had also been elected to the legislature, as had Mickey Leland, a dashing blue-eyed Black man in a dashiki who took Houston by storm.

I got to know Leland when he and I ended up as tokens of our race and gender in so-called leadership roles for Jimmy Carter's presidential campaign in 1976. Carter's Texas campaign was run by a small group of Georgia operatives who made Bob Armstrong the titular head of the Texas effort. But they needed a show of color and gender at the top and created titles for three co-chairs of the campaign. Mickey Leland was the token African American co-chair; Gonzalo Barrientos was the token Mexican American; and I was the token woman. In truth, we were given little responsibility in the campaign other than to keep up with our constituency groups, show up in the campaign office seven days a week, and give the appearance of working hard—a common practice of time-wasting "busy-work" that often sinks political campaigns. I guess we were somewhat effective in our rather limited roles, though, because Carter carried Texas in the 1976 election—something that no Democratic presidential candidate would be able to do for the next forty years and counting.

During the campaign, Mickey Leland and I had adjacent desks for our files and phones and had a lot of time to talk to each other. At some point, we began to talk about racial and ethnic identities, and he told me how he felt on his first trip to Africa. He had come alive there—seeing so many faces like his own in countries and cities run by people like him. He told me about walking the streets of Nairobi, talking to people in small villages in the countryside, and going for days without seeing a white face. The experience felt like some sort of psychic homecoming for him, an awakening of some deeper spirit that animated him and gave him a greater clarity about his own life and purpose. After Africa, he felt no need for his clenched-fist rhetoric to prove anything to himself or others, so he traded the dashiki for a pinstripe suit, wearing it with a bit of self-mockery and humor that made him the center of attention wherever he was. After Africa, a funny thing began to happen to a lot of white politicians who worked with Leland. They seemed uplifted rather than frightened or put off by his passionate rhetoric. His popularity soared. He was later elected to Congress when Barbara Jordan gave up her Houston congressional seat to return to Texas. A trained pharmacist, Leland then spent most of his congressional career on health and hunger issues. He took a lead role in securing $800 million for food and humanitarian relief supplies to ease famine in Ethiopia and Sudan in 1985.

Leland's insights opened a wider world for me and helped me understand on a deeper level the pivotal and very personal issues of race and identity. After he was killed in a plane crash in Ethiopia in 1989, three governors, two Speakers of the House of Representatives, and a host of other dignitaries paid homage to him at a memorial service in the Texas Capitol. That would never have happened before Africa. I later got to know his young widow, Alison Leland, who was left to care for their three young children. When Ann Richards became governor, she appointed Alison to the governing board of Texas A&M University, making her the first African American to serve in that important role.[3]

After the 1976 presidential campaign, my political efforts became more focused. I wanted to branch out. The nascent women's movement was growing, and our small group of friends and fellow activists was in the thick of it. In 1977, along with Jane Hickie and Claire Korioth, I helped conduct political campaign techniques workshops for women who were among the 2,000 delegates and 15,000 observers at the National Women's Conference in Houston.[4] My old Texas friend Betsey Wright, who now headed the Washington-based National Women's

Education Fund, brought me in to conduct workshops for female candidates and create campaign materials for several national labor unions. Under the auspices of the National Women's Education Fund, I was also able to spend a little time helping on a media project at Spellman College, a historically Black college for women in Atlanta. And that experience was another opportunity to gain a better understanding of the reality of Black lives in America. Yet, with all my national travels, I was still rooted in home and family . . . and local politics.

John had enthusiastically supported my new consulting activities and continued to encourage me to seek new opportunities, as he was doing. He had left the state AFL-CIO to run political campaigns and branch into other ventures. To our surprise, these new career efforts also created more opportunities for him to expand his own involvement in the lives of our adolescent children. He frequently ran a carpool for Eleanor, and he coached Billy's basketball games. He took the kids to the doctor or dentist while I was out of town. These actions, and other simple acts of basic childcare, earned him new respect among the women he worked with in politics. Something new was happening in the culture, and our marriage was evolving with the changing times to the benefit of both of us.

Turning Point

In 1978, after orchestrating a surprising upset victory that allowed Texas attorney general John Hill to defeat incumbent governor Dolph Briscoe in the Democratic primary, John ran straight into the new Republican juggernaut that helped launch young Karl Rove's career as a direct-mail guru and major political operative. John's candidate—heavily favored John Hill—suffered an ignominious defeat in the November general election at the hands of former Nixon deputy secretary of defense Bill Clements. This was the first time a Republican had been elected governor since Reconstruction. It was a humiliating loss for Democrats and for John personally. Although few recognized it at the time, Clements's campaign rode the first wave of right-leaning evangelical political involvement in Texas that would become more influential, and intensely cultivated by Rove, in subsequent Republican victories. After Clements's election, it would also become apparent that his personal oil fortune was underwriting the growth of the modern Republican Party of Texas, which made possible George W. Bush's rise to power sixteen years later and a humiliating defeat of my own with Ann Richards's loss of the governor's office.

John was wiped out and devastated after the loss. Losing the "big" one does something to your psyche—particularly if you're the campaign manager or *jefe* in charge. All the blame for a losing effort rests on you—no matter how many factors actually contributed to the loss—the vagaries of the candidate, the shifting demographics, the strength or money and savvy of the opponent, and, yes, . . . your own failure to prevent an unfolding disaster. As the old Notre Dame football coach Knute Rockne used to say, one loss is good for the soul. Too many losses are not good for the coach. Coaches, even political ones, have to jump back quickly to stay in the game. And the game was John's life. Fortunately, other opportunities allowed him to jump back into a new campaign rather quickly.

John and Jack Martin, a perceptive young former aide to US senator Lloyd Bentsen who had worked with John on Hill's governor's race, set up a partnership to continue their involvement in political campaigns.[5] Their first successful venture was an Austin race to elect then-Democrat Carole Keeton McClellan the first female mayor of Austin.[6] That victory led to still another one in Austin. They ran a $216-million bond campaign in 1979 to continue support for Austin's involvement with the South Texas Nuclear Project. Austin's rapid growth was creating a demand for additional electrical power, but the city had a small contingent of antinuclear activists who were bitterly opposed to nuclear power. Many of my friends were against the bond issue, and I also was ambivalent about the city's reliance on nuclear energy. One of my more radical friends asked me—seriously—if I was going to divorce John because of his role in this campaign. I was more amused than alarmed by the question at the time because John and I had made too many adjustments in our marriage over the years to let a policy or tactical disagreement break our bond. My answer was simply: "Are you kidding?"

The seriousness of the antinuke efforts was often undermined by the naiveté of a group of radical students and old Austin hippies who liked to snake-dance into City Council chambers wearing weirdly designed green-dragon costumes that were supposed to represent a nuclear monster. At the time, Austin was not afraid of the monster.

With a coherent strategy, money, a barrage of television ads, and massive mailings, John and Jack managed to persuade a slim majority of Austin voters to support the bonds. One of the most progressive communities in the country became a nuclear-power city. It was a surprising victory considering that the near-meltdown at the Three Mile Island nuclear power plant near Harrisburg, Pennsylvania, had occurred only a few weeks earlier, and it looked like support for nuclear-generated power was declining rapidly. Even John had doubts about the ultimate victory. However, an unexpectedly heavy turnout among voters in North Austin who still supported the project offset the antinuclear vote, which was mainly centered in student neighborhoods around the University of Texas.

John's friend Arthur "Buddy" Temple, a liberal state legislator from East Texas and later a railroad commissioner who regulated the Texas oil and gas industry, thought John had pulled off a miracle and started calling him "Nuke." The second nickname prevailed over the first one. John became less "Extremo" and more of a political seer who could pull off impossible wins, feats he repeated throughout the late 1970s and 1980s.

Shifting Political Winds

John and Jack Martin continued to develop their expertise in running political campaigns and were in the forefront of those who had figured out how to break the stranglehold that old-line Texas Democratic conservatives had always enjoyed in the state Senate. They recruited bright young candidates from all across the state to take on the old Senate bulls in newly drawn districts where they were vulnerable. All it took was a few dramatic defeats of the old guard to turn the Senate into a progressive echo chamber that began to uproot Texas's outdated and racist policies.

During the late 1970s, a new progressive alliance was forming that included not only organized labor and trial lawyers, African American and Mexican American political organizations, but also newly energized teachers, community organizations, environmental groups, and activists who were emerging from the newly minted women's movement. Texas progressives now had enough strength, particularly in the Texas Senate, to kill if not pass key legislation. John was in the thick of these efforts.

During that period, John also focused on changing the composition of the Texas Supreme Court. Judges in Texas are elected, and John and his partners began running nontraditional, aggressive statewide campaigns for progressive lawyers who wanted to be on the state's highest court. Establishment judges, supported by powerful business and legal elites, rarely had to worry about their elections, so they were blindsided by the victories of liberal justices. For a brief time, liberal-labor activists like former state senator Oscar Mauzy and civil rights lawyer Bill Kilgarlin dominated the court's swing toward progressive decisions more favorable to labor unions, minorities, and working folks.

Texas had already chalked up a roster of progressive reforms by the early 1980s. The new era was enhanced and expanded after the election of the liberal "Gang of Four" to statewide office in 1982. With money and organizational assistance provided by US senator Lloyd Bentsen and Texas lieutenant governor William P. Hobby, who were running for reelection, Jack Martin developed and ran a coordinated get-out-the-vote operation for the Democratic slate. Individual liberal candidates had also managed to raise enough money to run credible personal campaigns on their own. The combination of efforts managed to knock off all of the old conservative statewide Democratic officeholders. It was an unprecedented electoral coup for the progressives, who would shape Texas policies and politics for the next decade.

The new alliance helped take four dynamic new liberals to victory—dubbed the Gang of Four by the media. The combination of money, organization, and political savvy helped Ann Richards to become state treasurer. Jim Mattox, a former Democratic member of Congress from Dallas, became attorney general. Young Garry Mauro, a former Ralph Yarborough aide, became land commissioner after Bob Armstrong decided not to run for reelection. The biggest surprise of all was the election of Jim Hightower, the fiery populist *Texas Observer* editor, as agriculture commissioner.

Bob Bullock, a brilliant but often erratic and mercurial nonideological Democrat, had been elected state comptroller several years earlier and had set the pace for how a state agency could embark on serious reform and technology updates. Bullock served as a mentor to many of the new officeholders. His reforms provided a model for the new officials, who quickly set about to change the agencies they headed.[7]

Ann Richards reorganized the State Treasury's antiquated financial, investment, and money management systems, automating everything from check processing to basic accounting and investment procedures. As attorney general, Mattox became an aggressive consumer and anti-corporate advocate. As land commissioner, Mauro created an "Adopt a Beach" program to preserve Texas's endangered beaches along the Gulf Coast. As agriculture commissioner, Jim Hightower supported the growth of organic crop production and direct marketing of products by small farmers.

The Democratic sweep had major policy as well as procedural implications for the state. After moderate attorney general Mark White won the governor's race, defeating incumbent Republican Bill Clements in that 1982 election, he teamed up with Bill Hobby to get the legislature to pass the most far-reaching public-school reform package that Texas had seen since World War II. Governor White had persuaded business entrepreneur Ross Perot to head a statewide commission that recommended funding for public-school kindergartens, bilingual education, and the infamous "no-pass, no play" rule that began emphasizing academics over athletics in the state's high schools. They also dramatically increased state funding for local schools as well as for higher education. Ernesto Cortes's grassroots organizations in San Antonio and the Rio Grande Valley played a major role in generating public support for the education reforms.

While the overall reform package was popular, many Texas football fans hated the "no-pass, no-play" rule that required athletes, band members, and even cheerleaders to make passing grades in every course each six weeks or forego participation in extracurricular activities. The initial implementation of the rule hit rural high school football teams particularly hard. Republican Bill Clements capitalized on anger in rural and suburban communities to defeat Mark White in 1986 to regain the governor's office. Clements would stay in power until he had his fill of the Democratic-controlled legislature and the liberals who held statewide office. His decision not to run for reelection in 1990 set the stage for Ann Richards to become governor of Texas. But John Rogers would not see that day.

A Legacy

John's life was full. He was doing exactly what he wanted to do—just as his cancer surgeon had predicted four years earlier. Even though his appearance had changed, he could work and think and raise all the hell he wanted. He obviously enjoyed becoming more like the old El Extremo from his San Antonio days. John had never lost his copy editor's touch for sensational headlines and gossipy stories and had teamed up with former *Dallas News* reporter Sam Kinch and George Phenix, a former staffer for Senator Bentsen, to start a new political newsletter, *Texas Weekly*. His Thursday evening "work sessions" with the guys were one of the high points of his busy life.[8] He went to his office every day to strategize and strengthen the role of the labor movement and other progressive groups in the midst of new opportunities that were unfolding with the Gang of Four in power and a new generation of liberal and minority activists who were increasingly making their mark in the Texas legislature. Our son, Billy, was working with him on various

John Rogers had an intensity and energy that infused his personal and political life. A former journalist, he became a respected behind-the-scenes political strategist and advocate for the rights of workers and others fighting for dignity and equality. Surviving cancer, he died from an asthma attack in 1987.

projects, as was my younger brother, Frank Coniglio, who had moved to Austin and lived with us for a short time.

John was enjoying every minute of his political ventures, but it wasn't long before the debilitating aftereffects and recurring pain from his facial surgery began to limit his activities. In late October 1987 I knew something was different.

John was more fatigued than usual, often sinking into an exhausted silence when he came home in the evening. The severity of his asthma attacks was increasing. We had to cut short our twenty-seventh wedding anniversary dinner and leave our expensive meal untouched because something in the restaurant triggered an attack that made his breathing extremely difficult. That night, he adamantly refused to let me take him to the hospital for emergency relief. No more hospitals for him, he insisted. On some level, he seemed resigned to his declining health, but he was still working every day. Although I was beginning to realize that he was on a downward trajectory, I was still profoundly shocked when he died during the night three weeks later during one of those devastating asthma episodes.

John was only fifty-two years old when he died. The modern progressive era in Texas was in its prime. Ann Richards's election to the governor's office in 1990 would be both its culmination and the beginning of its demise. Although John missed the huge breakthrough of her election and the last few years of liberal influence on Texas politics and policy advancement, I always felt that it was part of his legacy. Others did too.

Political writer Dave McNeely described the packed crowd at John's memorial service at Austin's First United Methodist Church as a virtual "who's who" of Democratic politicians in Texas because John had worked for—or against—so many of them.[9] Although I was a member of the church, John most definitely was not. But senior pastor Dr. Jack Heacock knew John and fully understood that he had little use for organized religion. The pastor's remarks indicated that John's actions in the field of life were more important than sitting in the front pew when it came to admittance to heaven. He closed his remarks by reading a passage from the Book of Amos (5:23–24) about rejecting pomp and ceremony in favor of "straight-ahead pursuit of what's right."

> Take away from Me the noise of your songs;
> I will not even listen to the sound of your harps.
> But let justice roll down like waters,
> And righteousness like an ever-flowing stream.

That was John: rarely distracted by the noise of songs or the sound of harps. As his close friend attorney Charles "Lefty" Morris said, John's "passion to right what he saw as social wrongs through the political process was the central cohesive force of his activities."[10] Shortly after his death, the capital press corps dedicated its annual Gridiron Show, a satirical take on Texas politics, to John's memory. His friends set up a small memorial fund in his name to encourage the kinds of social and investigative journalism projects that he cared about. I think John would have been both surprised and proud.

Grief

While I had always been independent, John was my most reliable sounding board for whatever wild project I might consider. He was the smartest person I knew, my companion on the path we had chosen together. Still, I was surprised at the depths into which grief can penetrate. In those first few months after John's death, I didn't know how to come to terms with the loss I was feeling.

After a loved one dies, therapists often tell you that you have to go through a year of seasons to settle your grief. Holidays and significant anniversaries may trigger forgotten memories that resurrect the deep moments of shock and raw sorrow you felt in those first weeks after your loss. We who are bereaved are advised to prepare for these recurring episodes of fresh grief. But preparation is not prevention. And deep mourning could not be stifled or counseled away. Yet I learned to survive fairly intact during that first year without John, and I was not alone in my grief. I had the loving support of my adult children and my wonderful family. I had a wide circle of friends who encouraged and stood by me—leaving cupcakes at my front door, or arranging a massage, or taking me to a concert. Although I could no longer afford to live in our wonderful stone home in the hills, I was able to move to a smaller charming old house in the Rosedale neighborhood in central Austin.

Even though reality had already begun to penetrate the reflection of the sun and moon on the surface of the well of Texas politics before John died, I was learning that life has a way of opening new paths through the darkness. I was lucky to find a new path. After all, I had a job with the most interesting politician in Texas, who was riding a crest of progressive politics in our conservative state. I started over.

Women

How can you ensure that the progressive ventures that shaped you are accurately portrayed in the history of your times?

This is a particularly important point for women in Texas and for those of us who helped Ann Richards become governor. Traditionally, women's stories have been ignored, twisted, satirized, stereotyped, or grossly misunderstood. Our accomplishments have often been underestimated or minimized, notwithstanding our minimal efforts to turn the tide in our favor. That is certainly true in the stories told about Ann Richards, who is rarely placed within the historical context of her times. She is somehow trapped in popular history as a big-haired, tough-talking, cool mama.

That was only a small part of the story. And if the whole story is never told, who is to blame?

WHEN I FIRST JUMPED FULL-FORCE into San Antonio politics in the 1960s, most of the women I knew were like my mother—volunteers who made the phone calls, prepared the mailings, served punch at the events, and handed out slate cards at voting locations on election day. If they were really active, they might become delegates to the state or national Democratic Party convention. A peculiar type of enforced equality had emerged in 1948 when the national party established rules that required each state to have a female and male member of the Democratic National Committee (DNC).[1] For a woman, that was about as high as you could go in party politics, even though women could sometimes dominate comparable state and local executive committees.

The scarcity of women in elected office in Texas and elsewhere seemed unconsciously to limit our aspirations. Although Maine Republican Margaret Chase Smith was a long-serving member of the

US Senate, she was too remote to be a role model for me or other women activists in Texas.[2]

Texas actually had one woman serving in the state Senate in the 1960s, although she kept such a low profile that few had ever heard of her—including me! Neveille Colson had originally been elected to the state legislature back in 1939, to fill her dead husband's seat, the most common way for a woman to hold high office. That particular political phenomenon even had a name: "the widow's succession." Few women of my generation aimed to hold office in that manner.

The Dragon Ladies

When young women like me entered San Antonio's volatile political world, it wasn't particularly unusual for a woman to manage a campaign office or participate in planning meetings. But our voices were most often muffled by our own reticence rather than by any formal stricture. If we were bold enough to throw out an idea, it would usually be ignored until one of the men in the meeting casually repeated it as if it were his original suggestion.

There were always a few women, however, who rose to higher levels in our political world. They often had wealth and a particular kind of ambition to propel their husbands, sons, or brothers to greater levels of power and prestige. Those women usually had a "look"—perfect hair, long manicured nails, and fastidious outfits, if not overtly fashionable in a *Vogue* magazine sort of way. Their pristine appearance and a manipulative manner of operation accorded them a status that mere volunteers like me would probably never achieve. I used to call them the dragon ladies, because they could be ferocious if you ever had to tangle with them. Some of these women were masters of intrigue and knew how to use political gossip like a guided missile to target their perceived enemies or preserve their small bits of territory, even if it was only a local club, access to a particular male politician, or a coveted seat on the state party's executive committee.

Dragon ladies had a raptor-like focus on their goals. Expert vote counters, they seemed to have an uncanny ability to spot a weakness or opening that would allow them to move in on their prey—usually with such saccharine sweetness that you didn't know you had been attacked until it was all over.

I didn't have the skills, money, or ambition to be a dragon lady. I soon learned to stay out of their way, having been burned a time or two when I inadvertently stepped into their perceived territory within some political campaign. When I first encountered these backstage power brokers in the 1960s, I was probably intimidated as well as a tad jealous. They operated with an intensity and energy that I did not possess when my children were young. Now older and more experienced, I have some empathy (if not affection) for these women because they were trapped in a cultural and political system that accorded them few avenues to pursue their own ambitions. They had simply found a way to stay on top in a political world that they loved as much as I did. Still, when we moved to Austin and the wider world of Texas politics, it was not these powerful, backstage women I wanted to know. For me, the most compelling women in Austin were the free thinkers who were beginning to emerge from the male-dominated political world in which they had been as trapped as the dragon ladies.

The Fifties Girls

Ann Richards could be considered one of the glamorous Fifties Girls, the interesting women I wanted to know when we moved to Austin. A few years older than me, they were of the generation born in the 1930s that grew up in the 1940s, finished college in the early 1950s, and blazed out into the world in the 1960s, supporting the men who were the state's most flamboyant literary or liberal political figures. On the fringes of everything liberal in Texas, they were the smart, sexy housewives and muses to the brilliant men they married and whose children they bore. They seemed to be perfect mothers who could also hold their liquor, give sparkling parties, and be "worthy" companions to the decidedly Fifties Guys they loved.

Nadine Eckhardt, who had been married to two of those brilliant men, coined the term "Fifties Girls." She was prompted by the Texas writer Don Graham, who thought a book should be written about smart women like Nadine who came to maturity before the advent of the Second Wave Women's Movement and gave up the idea of a serious career for the sake of their husbands. The Fifties Girls were educated, bright, often beautiful and seemed content—at least on the surface—to live in a man's world. I would learn only later that many of these talented women took to booze or extraneous love affairs to mask their boredom and frustrations.

Nadine lived in that world, first during her marriage to the quintessential Texas novelist Billy Lee Brammer and later when she was married to liberal congressman Bob Eckhardt. Although Nadine had a number of interesting and important political jobs in Washington and managed the career of her illustrious second husband, she grew increasingly frustrated within the confines of her marriage and work. So it is not surprising that it was Nadine who wrote the book that Don Graham had suggested. In her wonderful memoir, *Duchess of Palms*, she described her role as a sidekick in politics and her own personal growth to escape it.[3] She told the story of women of her generation who loved the political life but could not easily make it their own.

By the early 1980s some of the cleverest of the Fifties Girls had broken the mold to become liberated feminists and accomplished writers or politicians on their own. They left a lot of distinguished men in their wake. Take Celia Morris, who showed up in Nadine's book and later became a friend of mine after she wrote a book about Ann Richards's 1990 election campaign.[4] Celia was first married to the acclaimed writer Willie Morris and later to Nadine's ex, Bob Eckhardt. Then she discarded them both and became a feminist scholar and successful writer on her own.

When I first got to know Ann Richards in Austin, she was of the generation that had not quite thrown off all the conventions of the fabulous Fifties Girls. She was married to brilliant civil rights attorney David Richards. While she was as consumed by politics as David was, Ann's primary role was as his helpmate and mother to their four children. Ann organized their lives, carried her unique sense of humor into all sorts of madcap adventures, planned their parties, and drank and caroused with David and the glittering group of hell-raising lawyers, writers, and musicians who mocked the conservative icons who ruled the state. She was the great entertainer of liberal, literary Austin and cooked gourmet meals, collected art, and raised chickens in order to have access to real "farm" eggs. She did it all—perfectly!

To her great credit, by the time the 1980s rolled around, Ann Richards had emerged from that fifties fog without the booze—or a husband. Her remarkable sense of humor was intact, and she launched into a new political life that would ultimately shape my own. Perhaps because she had once embraced then consciously dropped those self-destructive Fifties Girls experiences, she was able to bring something astonishingly unique to Texas politics: her true, aware, uninhibited self.

A Movement?

When Ann Richards and our like-minded friends came together in the early 1970s, we didn't know we were part of something historians would soon call the Second Wave Women's Movement. We just knew we wanted to play a role in changing Texas. Subtle shifts in power had already begun with the passage of the Civil Rights and Voting Rights Acts in the mid-1960s. The doors were opening not only for people of color but for women as well.

I was excited to take part in the organizational meetings of the Texas Women's Political Caucus in 1971 because we believed we were breaking new ground for women—at least in Texas. In 1972 young Austin attorney Sarah Weddington was elected to the Texas House of Representatives, and two years later Wilhelmina Delco, an accomplished Austin African American educator, joined her in the state house. In 1976 Ann Richards got herself elected Travis County commissioner, a member of the governing entity that contained the city of Austin and several smaller cities within its boundaries.

We didn't know that other Texas women had won similar elections to various county and city offices as far back as the 1920s. Somehow their stories hadn't even achieved footnote status in the prevailing Texas history textbooks that shaped our education and knowledge of our state. But women were not the only omissions in our standard history.

The history that my generation learned in Texas segregated public schools glorified Sam Houston's victory over the Mexican General Antonio López de Santa Anna at the Battle of San Jacinto but didn't teach us how deeply Houston wanted to preserve the Union or how he fought unsuccessfully to prevent Texas's secession and was removed as governor by the legislature because he refused to fight for the Confederacy.

We learned how the "awful" Yankee carpetbaggers treated white Southerners during Reconstruction after the Civil War, but we didn't learn about the impact of racist Jim Crow segregation laws and the legacy of slavery that kept a third of the Texas population destitute and terrorized by the Ku Klux Klan after Reconstruction.

We learned about the brave Texas Rangers who brought law and order to the Wild West, but we didn't learn about the brutality of individual Rangers toward Mexican Americans on the Texas border.

We might have been vaguely aware of the "Indian Wars" but never knew the details of how Native American tribes in Texas were so brutally wiped out.

Until I was well into adulthood, I never knew that Texas had a radical tradition that included an official Populist Party that fielded statewide candidates as well as a Socialist Party and Greenback Party. I had never learned about the Farmers Alliance that fought railroad and bank monopolies that were driving them into land foreclosures and bankruptcy. I didn't know that Black dock workers had gone on strike in Galveston to organize a union in the 1870s, and I never fully understood that the Texas legislature and a few progressive governors had enacted an array of friendly laws for workers—railroad safety measures, workers' accident compensation, mine-safety codes, farm crop distribution networks, and perhaps more importantly laws that protected debtors from losing their homesteads to repay banks or loan sharks or

The Texas Women's History Project, sponsored by the Foundation for Women's Resources, developed a traveling museum exhibition in the 1980s that visited major cities like San Antonio, Austin, Dallas, Houston, and Amarillo. The exhibit, "Texas Women: A Celebration of History," was organized and developed by a small staff, which included (from left to right) Ruthe Winegarten, Janelle Scott, me, Sherry Smith, Melissa Hield, Frieda Werden, and Mary Sanger. (Photo courtesy of Alan Pogue)

others who tended to exploit them. However, it was the shock of discovering bits of the history of women in Texas that galvanized us into meaningful statewide political action.

The Lost Women

When we began our statewide Women's History Project in the early 1980s, most serious scholars who specialized in Texas history were male and seemed to be perpetually intrigued by those brave defenders of the Alamo or the oil tycoons and cattle ranchers and the politicians who did their bidding. Most of them were oblivious to the quite different histories experienced by former slaves, Mexican families that were here before the first Anglos arrived, and the exploited workers who tried to form labor unions. And the women . . . well, how could we have expected the historians of the time to focus on busybody women with their do-gooder political goals in the 1920s? They simply didn't fit the conventional patterns of Texas history.

Activist women were just an aberration, a historical blip that could be easily ignored or dismissed outright. It was only natural that our group of friends knew nothing about these pioneering political women and the Texas suffrage movement and not at all surprising that the prevailing attitude about them was exemplified by a male member of the Texas legislature, who told one of those do-gooder women who had come to visit him about a piece of legislation to simply go home and darn her husband's socks.

When our crew began to piece together the fragments of women's lives in early Texas for our museum exhibition "Texas Women: A Celebration of History," we discovered a bevy of policy achievements led by women from the 1880s until well into the 1930s.

After the Civil War, well-to-do white women had created an effective prohibition movement that outlawed the sale of alcohol in Texas, complementary to the national effort to enact the 18th Amendment to the US Constitution. Emboldened by their success, many of these women moved quickly into the already existing woman suffrage movement. The Texas state constitution in 1876 said that all men could vote except "persons under twenty-one," "idiots and lunatics," "paupers," and "persons convicted of any felony." Women were not even mentioned. But with incredible drive and surprisingly sophisticated political skills, these women quickly won the right to vote in state Democratic primary elections in 1918, even before the federal 19th Amendment became law in 1920. Although a shameful compromise with racist legislative leaders effectively left Texas Black women out of the effort, more than 386,000 white Texas women registered to vote in only seventeen days between the passage of the state primary suffrage law and the 1918 election.[5] In the infamous "white primary," their votes helped the somewhat reluctant suffrage supporter William Hobby defeat one of the most controversial and colorful governors in Texas history, James Ferguson. The women didn't stop there.

A coalition of women's organizations, including the Federation of

Women's Clubs, Parent Teacher Association, League of Women Voters, Woman's Christian Temperance Union, and Business and Professional Women's Associations, banded together to create the Joint Legislative Council. The coalition advocated a long list of humanitarian changes affecting women and children, including emergency appropriations to fund Texas public schools, the enactment of stronger child labor laws, and the much-needed reform of Texas's brutal prison system. One legislator was so outraged by their program that he called it "the most audacious piece of Bolshevism ever permitted to clutter up this chamber."[6] The press was equally derisive, dubbing the women's groups "the Petticoat Lobby." Minnie Fisher Cunningham, Jane Y. McCallum, and others happily took up the moniker and became volunteer lobbyists who harassed and cajoled lawmakers to finally pass their legislative agenda, which also included strong infant and maternal health care services, free textbooks, prohibitions on child labor, and a system of local public libraries all across the state.

Largely because of Cunningham's political organizing skills in the 1918 general election, female voters and their organizations put Annie Webb Blanton in charge of the state's public education system, making her the first woman elected statewide in Texas. Dozens of other women won election to local and county offices in Texas as well as to the state House and Senate. Women were also serving on school boards, in city councils, and even as members of the state legislature, and 109 of the state's 254 county treasurers were women by 1929. Until we unveiled our Texas Women's History Project in 1980, however, few knew their names or their stories, still deemed relatively unimportant by many Texas myth-perpetuating male historians. Even so, many of these unknown women ushered in a new humanitarian era for Texas. Some of their reforms allowed later progressives to build upon their efforts.

World War II drove many of these activist women into the workforce, and the rest faded into their unknown histories. One notable female attorney, however, continued to struggle almost alone for years to expand the rights of women in Texas law and policy. After Texas voters approved a state constitutional amendment in 1954 to allow women to serve on juries, one of the leaders of the effort, Hermine

Tobolowsky, became known as the "mother of equal rights." Yet it took her until 1967 to get the legislature to allow women the right to control their own property without securing permission from their husbands. And she continued to lay the legal groundwork that finally got Texas to add an Equal Rights Amendment to the state constitution. Although most women like Hermine Tobolowsky were forgotten, their humanizing influence remained.

When we began our research to find the lost women in Texas history, we made a conscious decision to focus on more than politics. We were influenced by some of the first American historians who were doing seminal work on the history of women. Because of feminist historians like Gerda Lerner and Eleanor Flexner, we looked deeper into what was going on within evolving Texas communities as well as in frontier Texas.[7] We discovered the stories of long-ignored cultural icons, community builders, business entrepreneurs, ranch owners, educators, artists, athletes, civil rights leaders, and significant philanthropists who funded hospitals and schools. One of them, Clara Driscoll, heiress to her family's ranching and banking fortune, became known as the "savior of the Alamo" because she purchased properties adjacent to the site and supported the state's decision to bequeath the site to the Daughters of the Republic of Texas to maintain for posterity. This saved the Alamo from rank commercialism and possible destruction.

For the first time, we could also reveal the stories of several dozen women of color like Jovita Idar and Christia Adair, who might have been known in their own communities but had never been included in any general history of Texas.[8] We actually pulled one of those women out of obscurity to give her the kinds of positive accolades that she deserved for the risks she had taken and the struggles she led.

"La Pasionaria de Texas"

I had heard of the mysterious Emma Tenayuca, "La Pasionaria," when John and I were involved in San Antonio politics.[9] Almost everyone we knew in the labor movement seemed to have a story about her, but no one knew where she was or even if she was still alive. Mexican American activists considered her some sort of romantic hero because she had led almost twelve thousand Latina pecan shellers out on strike in 1938 to protest wage cuts and abysmal working conditions in dusty sheds where the workers were mostly women and the cracking and shelling was done by hand. She seemed lost to history.

Tenayuca's legend only grew with the passage of time. But it took our Women's History Project's intrepid researcher, Ruthe Winegarten, only a couple of weeks to locate the legendary Emma Tenayuca in 1981. She was then a 65-year-old grandmother and retired public schoolteacher living quietly in a modest San Antonio neighborhood. Although few people really knew the details of her colorful past, many did know about the pecan shellers' strike because San Antonio was the commercial shelling center for the nation's pecan crop production in the 1930s, with almost 400 shelling factories in the area.

Southern Pecan Shelling Company was the largest owner in the area and paid its mostly female workforce five or six cents a pound for the shelled pecans. The company had recently cut wages even more. When the workers walked off the job to protest, young Emma Tenayuca stepped in to rally and encourage them, becoming the de facto leader of the strike. Although she was only twenty-two years old, she was already known in San Antonio as a labor organizer and had been arrested several times for her protests on behalf of poor Mexican American workers as well as for her involvement in a strike at a cigar-manufacturing facility. Because of her leadership in the radical Workers Alliance, a national organization formed by the Communist Party during the Great Depression, she was a target for the virulent anti-Communist local sheriff, who monitored her activities. Her marriage to Homer Brooks, a well-known Communist Party organizer, further tagged her as a radical agitator.

The pecan shellers' strike turned violent when picketers were gassed, arrested, and jailed. Yet workers eventually won a wage increase through a national arbitration process. The settlement didn't last long, however, because factory owners in the area soon mechanized the industry. Most of the female workers ultimately lost their jobs. Yet Emma Tenayuca's

Labor organizer Emma Tenayuca was one of the "lost women" of Texas history whose story was finally told in the exhibition "Texas Women: A Celebration of History." Here we are together at a Labor Day picnic in San Antonio in 1982.

leadership in the pecan shellers' strike, and the total disruption of the commercial pecan industry, made her a national figure. It also made her a target of leaders of the San Antonio business community, who made sure she never came near their employees. Although she continued to try to organize Mexican American workers, Tenayuca had become such a controversial figure that she was even shunned by many area labor leaders who wanted peace with local employers. Rumors spread that she was having difficulty finding any kind of work. She simply disappeared from the public eye, but not from the public's imagination.

After Ruthe Winegarten contacted Tenayuca, she was initially very suspicious about the motives of a bunch of Anglo women who wanted to tell her story. After all, she had been burned by excessive public scrutiny in her youth. However, she agreed to see me after she learned that I had been active in the tumultuous San Antonio politics of the 1960s. I drove to San Antonio one afternoon to persuade her to be involved in our project. She served me coffee and cake as we sat in her modest home and talked for hours about everything from San Antonio's current politics to the Los Angeles Dodgers, which she followed religiously because of her affection for ace Mexican pitcher Fernando Valenzuela. She was so warm and welcoming to me and interested in everything that was going on in Texas politics. During that afternoon, we formed the basis of a personal relationship that allowed her to trust us to be fair in telling her story. Later she wrote me a note to let me know that after our visit her "uneasiness had turned to great expectations."[10]

We did not want to disappoint her. We told Emma Tenayuca's story with bold visuals as well as an accurate narrative of her life and impact on the poor and easily discarded Mexican American women in San Antonio. In the 1940s, when she no longer felt safe and could not find a job, Tenayuca moved to California, enrolled in San Francisco State College, and earned a degree in education. She had divorced her husband, dropped her Communist Party affiliations, and taught school in California for ten years before she quietly returned to San Antonio, where she still had family. Back home, she earned her master's degree from Our Lady of the Lake University and taught in the Harlandale Independent School District, living quietly and anonymously until we found her.

Because of our inclusion of Emma Tenayuca in the women's history project, she was able to emerge from the shadows of Texas history to highlight an era of radical labor organizing at a traumatic time during the Great Depression. Ultimately, she was inducted into the San Antonio Women's Hall of Fame. In an oral history conducted for the Institute of Texan Cultures in 1987, Tenayuca said that for the first time in her life she felt like some sort of heroine because she had finally received recognition for her efforts as a labor organizer.

An Awakening

As we put together information on women like Emma Tenayuca and others, we knew we had important stories to tell. We began to meet with small groups of women all across the state to generate support for the project and more importantly to raise the funds to fabricate and tour the exhibition. We seemed to awaken some long-dormant need among so many women who wanted to know more about our unknown history. While most had never given money to any kind of women's project before, they wrote checks for $25 or $100 or more to support our efforts. However, the big surprise for us was the positive reaction of male business and political leaders we solicited in our fundraising. Rather than the skepticism we expected, we encountered curiosity and support. Many had stories to tell us about a favorite teacher who had been a major influence in their lives, or a grandmother who had fought for suffrage, or a talented daughter for whom they wanted to have the same opportunities as for their sons.

While Ann Richards was the chief motivator and leader of our efforts, it was the indefatigable Liz Carpenter who helped connect us with the kinds of celebrities who provided star power for our exhibit openings in major cities all over Texas. Liz simply fell in love with our project and pulled out all the stops to make it a reality.

Liz Carpenter had been Lady Bird Johnson's press secretary in the White House and remained close friends with her after they both came back to Texas. She brought Lady Bird Johnson into our fold, which gave our effort enormous creditability, particularly as we struggled to raise money to create our exhibits. Liz was a great "connector" who opened doors for us everywhere. She seemed to know bigwigs all over the country, whether they were in journalism, politics, or the entertainment industry. She did not hesitate to call them to help bring our project to life.

One Saturday morning, Jane Hickie hosted a brunch for Liz and our gaggle of close friends. She provided a wonderful buffet and an unlimited supply of chilled mimosas. Because she also had a new hot tub installed on her deck under the trees, the morning extended into early afternoon as we sat in a hot tub gossiping and drinking our mimosas. Liz obviously had a little buzz going and began calling her celebrity friends to enlist them in our cause. While Liz was in that hot tub, she convinced movie star Ginger Rogers and Broadway icons Mary Martin and Carol Channing to headline exhibit openings in San Antonio, Austin, and Dallas.

Lady Bird Johnson was a major supporter of the "Texas Women: A Celebration of History"
exhibition and was particularly interested in the panel that told how women from the
1880s onward created public libraries in almost every community in Texas. (Photo courtesy
of TWU Libraries' Women's Collection, Texas Woman's University, Denton, Texas)

But we also had the help of other connectors, who believed in what we were doing and were willing to host fundraising events or set up appointments with key donors for us. In Houston it was Diana Hobby. She was a civic leader and the wife of lieutenant governor William P. Hobby, the son of a former Texas governor and Oveta Culp Hobby, who had served as commander of the Women's Army Corps during World War II. When the Hobby family, the owners and publishers of the *Houston Post*, publicly supported our project, they opened the doors for some of Houston's wealthiest individuals to contribute to our effort. Our own close friend Katherine B. "Chula" Reynolds, a King Ranch heiress, brought in a group of strong Republican women from San Antonio who helped reinforce the nonpartisan nature of our efforts.

While it was our ace team of researchers who found and helped develop the stories of the lost women of our history, we could not have pulled off the feat without these important connectors and key donors.[11]

I realize that history always has a personal angle, and this is certainly mine. Yet something happened to all of us when we dug back into women's history. We began to understand that we were fulfilling the legacies of those progressive women of the 1920s and 1930s through our political activism. We felt an obligation not only to carry on their work but to expand and surpass it in our own political efforts. It was an impetus to further action. After the completion of the Texas Women's History Project in the 1980s, a new generation of female historians has continued to dig, discover, and write about the impact on the public life of remarkable Texas women who have rarely been noticed until now.

Our own Ruthe Winegarten published more than twenty books about the role of women in Texas's complicated history before she died in 2004. Even the Texas State Historical Association (TSHA), which is the voice of the state's history establishment, began to add new entries about long-neglected women into its venerable *Handbook of Texas*. TSHA began publishing an online *Handbook of Texas Women*, with hundreds of new entries about women who have been important in the overall history of our state. But Ellen Temple, who was part of our efforts from the beginning, has probably done more than any other individual to make women's history in Texas come alive. As a publisher and documentary filmmaker, she has encouraged and supported a new generation of women historians in their research and writing.

Nancy Baker Jones has been one of the most influential leaders in this effort.[12] Other prominent historians who have made their mark on Texas women's history include Judith McArthur, Jessica Brannon-Wranosky, Rachel Collins, Jacqueline Jones, Gabriela Gonzalez, Teresa Palomo Acosta, Merline Pitre, Fran Vick, Melissa Hield, and Cynthia Beeman. These female historians are influencing and providing valuable sources of information for a new generation of male historians and writers who are seriously trying to understand and write about women as they explore the realities of Texas's past rather than its glorious myths.

Yet many women of my generation have not yet told their own personal stories to round out this history and fill in the information gaps about the difficulty of achieving full legal and political equality for women in the 1970s and 1980s. Truth be told, the political roots for many of us who moved into Texas politics during those early years might surprise some of those male historians who now struggle to probe the history of women in Texas.

Many of us learned our politics by volunteering in the campaigns of a rather driven man who barely escaped being classified as one of those tiresome liberals who always ran and always lost campaigns to break into the conservative political establishment. One of those active volunteers in his campaigns—Governor Ann Richards—honored him with a huge reception at the Governor's Mansion on his ninetieth birthday. His name was Ralph W. Yarborough.

10

Roots

*He was quirky, eccentric, intense, and ferociously ambitious. And he was
bold enough to repeatedly challenge the most powerful men in Texas, who
ran the state as if it was their own personal fiefdom. They called him a
Communist who criminally advocated the mixing of the races and, even
worse, a labor stooge and perpetual loser. But he was "Our Ralph."*

*Many of us learned how to fight for just causes in Ralph Yarbor-
ough's chaotic campaigns. In the early days, he never won. And then he
did—finally.*

*On the very day that Yarborough won a hotly contested race for a
vacant United States Senate seat, I was a 16-year-old schoolgirl standing
in our backyard waiting for my parents to come home from voting. More
significantly for me on that day, however, I was anxiously watching the
western horizon as a dangerous tornado ripped through Dallas and began to
ascend back into the clouds above us.[1]*

*Thirteen years later, I was a paid staffer in Ralph Yarborough's losing
campaign to hold on to the Senate seat he won on that stormy day in
Dallas.*

I REMEMBER GOING WITH MY mother while I was still in high school
to a Sunday afternoon meeting of Ralph Yarborough supporters at the
home of labor organizers Don and Ruth Ellinger. Yarborough was an
old-time Texas populist district judge from East Texas who became
a liberal hero because he was a fearless challenger who relentlessly
attacked the powerful economic interests that ruled the state. Until
that stormy day in 1957 when he was victorious in the winner-take-all
special election to fill a vacant US Senate seat, however, Yarborough
had never been able to score enough votes to win the governor's office
that he always coveted. He had never been able to overcome charges

that he was a Communist sympathizer who advocated the "co-mingling" of the races that would lead to the "mongrelization" and decline of the white race. That was Texas then: blatant racism without subtlety or nuance and all out in the open.

The Yarborough meeting was the first time in my life that I had ever been in the same room with African American and Mexican American leaders. They were forming a statewide coalition with white liberals and labor leaders to bring Texas fighting and screaming into the modern era. Watching these adults work together had a lasting impact on me and shaped my conviction that this kind of diverse leadership was the way it *should* be in Texas politics. Ralph Yarborough became the most visible and quixotic leader around whom these new groups coalesced.

Yarborough's multidecade struggle to topple the political leadership that had nurtured the most conservative, reactionary, and racist elements in Texas society served as a training ground for a future generation of progressive leaders—particularly many women who came to political consciousness in the 1960s and early 1970s. Yarborough wasn't exactly a feminist, but most of us had probably not yet fully incorporated a coherent philosophy of feminism that could be manifest in our own lives. Ann Richards, Clair Korioth, Ruthe Winegarten, and others who became active in the women's movement started out as volunteers in his campaigns, as I did. We learned what politics was all about. We honed our skills in his campaigns and got to see authentic politicians in action. Mostly, we were drawn to Yarborough's anti-elitist, populist spirit that shaped liberal politics from the 1950s to the 1970s and beyond. His campaign slogan was "Put the jam on the lower shelf so the little man can reach it."[2] We just wanted the "little woman" to get some of it too.

An amazing group of little-known women was at the forefront of new progressive groups that coalesced around Yarborough. Labor organizers Latane Lambert and Rosa Walker led grassroots organizing efforts, as did Houston activists Billie Carr and Frankie Randolph. Also out front in those struggles were Dallas's civil rights leaders Erma LeRoy and Juanita Craft; San Antonio's Kathleen Voigt and Olga Peña; El Paso's Alicia Chacón; and other anonymous women who, like my mother, became loyal foot soldiers in the cause. One of them, Earlene Day, would gather teenage volunteers in her big East Dallas home to help get out mailings for Yarborough's campaigns. I thought it was so cool that she always served us little finger sandwiches and Cokes over ice in crystal glasses.

Yarborough was able to hold on to his Senate seat for thirteen years. He was instrumental in extending World War II GI benefits for Korean War veterans; he got Texas's wonderful Padre Island designated as a protected National Seashore Area; and he was the only senator from the Old South to vote for the Civil Rights Act of 1964 and the Voting Rights Act of 1965. Those votes probably helped contribute to the loss of his Senate seat in 1970.

I was twenty-nine years old when I "ran" Yarborough's San Antonio campaign headquarters for that losing Senate race. In truth, however, I was a mere office manager, never a decision-maker for the kind of campaign later described as antiquated Texas populism and post–voting rights activism. But Yarborough was already hopelessly outdated with both his message and the mechanics of his campaign. He was defeated not by one of those overt racist reactionaries he had fought all those years but by Lloyd M. Bentsen Jr., a moderate with deep ties to the conservative Democrats who controlled the party. Bentsen would rise in the US Senate and ultimately be the Democratic nominee for vice-president of the United States in 1988. In one of the great and wonderful ironies of Texas politics, Senator Bentsen would one day supplant Ralph Yarborough to become a hero to organized labor in Texas. And he helped many women like Ann Richards win public office. When I was chosen to hold the Lloyd M. Bentsen Jr. Endowed Chair in Business and Public Policy at the Lyndon B. Johnson School of Public Affairs at the University of Texas in the 1990s, I was honored and grateful.

Still, as I chalked up one more political loss in that Yarborough-Bentsen election, I was beginning to learn about what worked and what did not work in the bizarre world of Texas campaigns. The struggles would continue, with defeat after defeat over the years. But modern liberal politics in Texas did not start or end with old Ralph Yarborough. Much of it continued in the early 1970s with a particularly notable woman, who also provided opportunities for younger women like me to learn more, do more, and be more of who we wanted to be.

"Sissy"

I came under the spell of Frances "Sissy" Farenthold in a very personal way simply by running an errand requested by my husband.

In 1970 John Rogers and the AFL-CIO had been heavily involved with the Dirty Thirty reform movement in the Texas legislature after a huge stock fraud and bribery scandal involving the Sharpstown Bank in Houston resulted in a 50 percent turnover in both houses and ended the careers of a half-dozen high-level conservative Democrats. A few of them even went to jail.[3] Younger, more liberal leaders began to emerge, helped along by federal court decisions on voting rights that brought African Americans, Latinos, and even a few Republicans into power in that electoral sweep. But it was a bipartisan, ragtag bunch of state legislators dubbed the Dirty Thirty that brought serious reform to the state house. They got their name after a heated debate on the House floor when one of the few remaining old-guard legislators threatened to "get those thirty dirty bastards" who were blocking one of his bills. The name stuck. The reformers just dropped the word "bastards" and proudly started calling themselves the Dirty Thirty.[4]

Sissy Farenthold, the only woman member of the Texas House at that time, had become the "den mother" of the reformers who were changing the face of political power in Texas. Farenthold and state senator Barbara Jordan, the only woman and only African American in the state Senate, had sponsored Hermine Tabolowsky's long-fought equal legal rights amendment to the Texas Constitution, which voters passed overwhelmingly in a statewide election. After this and other notable breakthroughs, Farenthold became the most visible leader of the Dirty Thirty coalition.

Late one afternoon, John asked me to deliver some papers to Far-enthold's Capitol office on my way home from work in Bob Armstrong's nearby office. Her staff had already left for the day when I arrived, and she waved me into her inner office while she was on the phone. I overheard her telling her daughter to defrost the pork chops in the freezer so that she could fix dinner for her kids when she finally got home. At that moment, the heroic Sissy Farenthold became human for me—another working mom trying to hold it together, so human in her need to take care of her family and so totally engaged in waging public fights that she would only occasionally win. I guess one reason I came to like Sissy so much was because I had seen her in that unguarded moment, when her fragile image made me view her in a new light.

While women like me became her die-hard fans, Sissy's courage and fortitude made her the object of bitter hatred and vitriolic outrage from the conservative wing of the Democratic Party, which feared her growing influence and public appeal.

Frances "Sissy" Tarlton Farenthold of Corpus Christi grew up in a prominent Texas family of lawyers and judges. Following her family trajectory, she had been one of only eight female students who graduated from the University of Texas Law School in 1949. After she was elected to the state legislature in 1968, she became a force for civil rights and economic opportunity for poor women and children.

Because of widespread acclaim for her leadership role with the Dirty Thirty reformers, Sissy Farenthold quickly picked up the liberal mantle from old Ralph Yarborough to run for statewide office. Ever popular, she ran for governor twice. The first time she ran in the Democratic primary, she knocked off Ben Barnes, the lieutenant governor and John Connally–crowd favorite, as well as the incumbent governor, Preston Smith, ending their days in public office. She finished a surprisingly strong second in the primary and forced conservative rancher Dolph Briscoe into a party runoff.

During her primary runoff election, I had organized a big meeting in Austin to hear Sissy speak to an environmental organization. We had secured a place for the gathering at the First English Lutheran Church just a few blocks north of the University of Texas campus. Bob Armstrong was going to introduce Sissy, and we had arranged for a small band to play as people entered the meeting hall. We distributed flyers all through the area and even ran 30-second radio spots publicizing the event. As it turned out, that was a big mistake. One of the elders of the church had heard the radio ad and demanded that the pastor withdraw permission for us to use the facility. He was not going to allow "his" church to host that radical woman and allow her to spew her dangerous left-wing views. The hapless pastor called me the morning of the meeting to give me the news: we would have to cancel the meeting at his church. His call threw me into a state of absolute panic. I didn't know what to do. We were expecting several hundred people to attend our event.

In numerous pleading telephone conversations, I begged and badgered the pastor to reverse the church's decision and even had an unpleasant exchange with his conservative elder—all to no avail. Finally, calm Bob Armstrong stepped in to do what I could not. He simply arranged for a restaurant across the street from the church to let us use its outdoor garden for our event. All we had to do then was to put up new signs for directions to the meeting. We had a hugely successful gathering with an overflow crowd. I don't think Sissy or her staff ever knew of our problem.

Although the primary runoff election gave hope to Texas liberals all across the state, Sissy could not prevail. Conservative Dolph Briscoe defeated her, 55 to 44 percent. It was not yet time for a liberal woman to be elected governor of Texas.

Although I quickly moved on to other political adventures, I probably should have held on to the memory of the church-canceled event that I organized and agonized about earlier in Sissy's campaign. As it turned out, that episode represented the same sort of angry rejection and hatred that Ann Richards would face almost every day that she sat in the governor's office. I clearly held on to my illusions that our side could prevail, even against Texas's conservative establishment. But I was continuing to learn, particularly about my own weaknesses and strengths.

Between Sissy Farenthold's losing campaign and Ann Richards's winning campaign for governor in 1990, a lot was happening to bring women into political leadership throughout the state. By the time Ann was elected governor, women had become mayors of every major city in Texas. A new wave of women had been elected to the state legislature. Their ranks included Democratic liberals and Republican conservatives. In a relatively short-lived era of bipartisan cooperation in the 1980s, those women managed to work together on a number of policy issues that affected women. And their presence began to open doors for others to have a more meaningful political participation in the public life of our state. I learned from and revere them all. In his quirky, outdated way, "Our Ralph" helped us get there, as did a woman called Sissy.

PART IV

Threads

Politics

When I was about twelve years old, my parents took me to a small-dollar fundraiser for Democratic presidential candidate Adlai Stevenson, who was running a lost-cause campaign against World War II hero General Dwight David Eisenhower.

Over the summer months, my parents had dropped me off at the Stevenson headquarters in downtown Dallas to look up phone numbers of voters on precinct lists. It was kind of boring, but it gave me something to do that summer. I liked listening to the grownups talk about politics and the ups and downs of campaigning for liberal Stevenson in conservative Dallas. I was eager to attend the fundraising event in the Crystal Ballroom at the Baker Hotel, because it was all the staff in the campaign office talked about.

I loved being in the glittery ballroom with the jostling crowd. The clink of cocktail glasses, the buzzing gossip, and even the pallid speeches were thrilling to me. It seemed like so much fun to be with people who were having a good time and united in some sort of cause. Their excitement was infectious.

But was that really politics? Or was it simply a thread of excitement that generated a dream of something larger? Whatever it was, I was hooked—like some sort of addiction that played out over the years. However, as I grew older, I learned that what I was ultimately seeking was not merely excitement but something more authentic and meaningful. It was not easy to find.

MAYBE I DIDN'T REALLY HAVE an addiction to politics, at least as defined in clinical terms. Perhaps it was more like a compulsion. Whatever it was, it was so powerful that by the time I became a young adult I had absorbed my parents' notion that politics mattered and could be an important element in a purposeful life. In those early years, it was also fun and exciting enough to generate those addictive qualities of reward and relief, relapse and remission. I always wanted more . . . and more.[1]

As a kid, I loved driving around with my dad to put up political yard signs. As a young wife and mother, I had a great time in San Antonio at those raucous West Side political rallies. It was fun to caucus with the liberals at one of those wild state Democratic Party conventions in the early 1970s or to indulge in "big talk" about strategies or tactics. And because Ann Richards was such a sparkly and distinctive public figure, she was a magnet for all sorts of celebrities who wanted to know her. That added to the pure excitement of being part of her entourage. Excitement was always part of the package. It started very early in her public career for those of us lucky enough to be along for the ride.

Ann spoke at her first national Democratic convention in San Francisco in 1984—the one that nominated Geraldine Ferraro as vice-president in Walter Mondale's losing presidential effort. We were simply gaga when we were backstage and got to meet Warren Beatty, who was also speaking at the convention. After Ann's 1988 Democratic convention speech that made her a national celebrity and helped launch her campaign for governor, we were over the moon when Steven Spielberg, Robin Williams, Lily Tomlin, Don Henley, and especially Austin's own Willie Nelson put on benefits for her. Sure, those encounters were little more than mere sightings in the overall scheme of things in Texas. But they made us feel that we mattered and that our politics mattered too. There was more to come.

The Queen Comes to Texas

In 1991 Queen Elizabeth II of England and her husband Prince Philip, the Duke of Edinburgh, came to Texas. The purpose of her trip was to facilitate British investment opportunities and trade between the United Kingdom and Texas. At the time, the UK was the state's largest single source of foreign investment and already had significant relationships with the state's oil and gas producers. While in Texas, Queen Elizabeth and her entourage went to a rodeo in Houston and a fancy Dallas country club dinner. She also gave a speech to a joint session of the Texas legislature in Austin. Governor Richards hosted a

Queen Elizabeth spoke to a joint session of the Texas legislature while on a trade mission in 1991. Governor Ann Richards hosted her and Prince Philip, Duke of Edinburgh, at a special reception in the Governor's Mansion. The governor and Lady Bird Johnson later entertained the royal couple with a black-tie dinner. I also attended (seen here only from the back in my long white dress) and got to shake the queen's hand. (Photograph by Charles Guerrero)

reception for the royal couple at the Governor's Mansion, and she and Lady Bird Johnson arranged a black-tie dinner for them at the LBJ Presidential Library.

Our staff was caught up in a frenzy of excitement. My sister Martha Coniglio, who had a successful catering business in Dallas, came to Austin to help with protocol and other arrangements for the queen's visit. She worked with our friend Cathy Bonner, who could carry off all sorts of big deals, and Lavada Jackson Steed, who was the most respected arbiter of all things social in Austin. Lavada had organized most of Governor Richards's inaugural events a few months earlier. She and Martha were an impressive team of no-nonsense, detail-oriented event planners and party organizers. They had it under control. Our guest list for the black-tie dinner included about 100 members of Texas political and financial elites.

We knew that Prince Philip was a hunter and conservationist, so we wanted guests at his table to be conversant on these issues. Perry Bass, whose family held one of Texas's greatest oil fortunes, was a noted conservationist and sportsman as well as a sort of financial celebrity throughout Texas and the nation. Ann invited the elderly Bass and his wife to sit at the prince's table at the dinner.

A few days before the event, I got a call from Bass, then close to eighty years old. He seemed somewhat shy and said he was hesitant to impose on me. As it turned out, he was as excited to meet the queen and Prince Philip as we were. He wanted to be sure he knew what would be appropriate for him to do or say and even wear. Bass and I had a quite touching conversation, and he later sought me out at the dinner to thank me for my advice. He told me that this event was one of the highlights of his life.

Celebrity Connections Are Not Friendships

Perry Bass was a very nice conservative gentleman of the old school. If I had known him better, I'm sure I would really have liked him. What I was becoming increasingly conflicted about, however, was how the Bass money and connections gave him and his family such easy access to pomp and power, even when progressives like Ann Richards occupied the governor's office. It was clearly Bass's wealth and reputation that got him, and others, invited to meet the queen. Frankly, I have to admit that it was also quite exciting for perennial outsiders like us to find an occasion to hobnob with the richest people in Texas. So we had our own motives for inviting folks like Bass to the queen's dinner. At the time, I think we also somewhat naively hoped that powerful Texans like Perry Bass and others we cultivated would be unlikely to oppose Ann in the next election if they got to know us and understood what we were trying to do. Of course, these political connections that masquerade as friendships are entirely transactional and are dependent on the exchange of information, access, or money. Because so much of an officeholder's time has to be spent on fundraising, the art of cultivation is part of the game. You always need a lot of new "friends" if you want to remain in the office you hold. But assuming that these transactional connections could become true and loyal friendships is one more of the illusions we brought to the process of governing Texas. More importantly, it is a dangerous form of self-deception and denial in politics.

We would certainly learn that simple political truth less than two years later when Ann Richards's reelection campaign got underway. Sweet old Perry Bass supported George W. Bush when he ran against Ann. More disappointing to me than losing hope of earning the support of people like Bass was the defection of a few of our earliest supporters, who clearly had connections and interests that superseded their previous ties to Ann. One of those supporters put us on edge when he relayed a message from deep within the well of Perry Bass's family fortune.

When the governor's reelection campaign was entering its hottest and most intense phase in 1994, we had some information that might reveal the hypocrisy involved in George Bush's appeal to anti-abortion activists and the religious Right, who had become the most significant and cohesive bloc of solid Republican voters in our state. It was tangentially related to Bush's involvement with the Bass family's much-admired financial advisor, Richard Rainwater.

Rainwater's name kept cropping up in relation to George Bush's business dealings. He was one of the key investors who bought the Texas Rangers major league baseball team in 1989 and got taxpayers to help fund a magnificent new stadium in Arlington, between Dallas and Fort Worth. Rainwater put together the deal that allowed Bush to buy a 2 percent ownership stake as well as become managing partner for the team. The circumstances had always seemed a bit suspicious, because the son of the president didn't have any money of his own and had to borrow $600,000 to buy into the ball club. This ownership stake was the major source of Bush's personal wealth when he ran for governor. Shortly after Rainwater closed the deal to buy the Rangers, Bush paid off his loan by selling his stock in Harken Energy Company to a mystery buyer. The transaction had seemed unusual enough to warrant an investigation by the Securities and Exchange Commission, which ultimately took no action against Bush.[2]

Bush's involvement with the Rangers ball club and his newfound wealth seemed murky enough that Texas newspapers had covered the baseball story in detail early in the campaign, so we knew it no longer had any traction. But we still wanted to find out if there were other financial deals between Bush and his financial patron Richard Rainwater.

Rainwater had gotten his start when he began managing the Bass family's huge financial portfolio derived from the oil and gas ventures of the family patriarch, Sid Richardson, and his nephew and heir, Perry Bass. Thanks to Rainwater's savvy investments, particularly a well-publicized deal with the Walt Disney Company, the family fortune grew exponentially and made Bass and his four sons among the top 100 richest people in America at the time. When Rainwater later went out on his own, some of the companies he helped fix or create included Columbia/HCA Healthcare, the nation's largest for-profit health care system, as well T. Boone Pickens's Mesa Petroleum Company. He also facilitated Eddie Lampert's control of Sears Roebuck. Along the way, Rainwater's largesse had benefited not only George W. Bush but also Florida's then-governor Rick Scott, who at one time ran Rainwater's Columbia/HCA's large network of hospitals and later became a US senator.

Our research staff had discovered that Rainwater's vast financial empire also included extensive gaming interests and big casino ties. Even more significantly in terms of Texas politics, however, Rainwater's HCA Healthcare network was a provider of thousands of abortions each year, a fact that neither Rainwater nor anti-abortion candidate Bush wanted to be known in Texas. While we were still trying to figure out what we might do with this information, we got a call from a Houston investment banker who was a longtime supporter of Ann's. He let us know that he was a close friend of Rainwater's and that we'd have hell to pay if we "dragged" Rainwater or his holdings into the political campaign against Bush. I wasn't sure if this was blustery rhetoric on behalf of a friend or a threat. Either way, it was a disturbing call. In the final days of the campaign, however, we were so busy fighting off the Bush campaign's attacks on Ann that we didn't have the time or resources to pursue the Rainwater connection, whatever it might have been.

After the campaign ended and I retreated back into academia, I continued to be on alert whenever Rainwater's successes in the financial world hit the news. He seemed to have a magic touch. The business press covered his every move and his big money deals, of which there were many. Although it was hard for me to grasp the extent or complexity of his Wall Street successes, I was fascinated by his ventures and his ties to the most powerful people in the nation.[3]

All of my previous experiences within the nexus of politics and money had to do with small-ball city politics or the hurly-burly hustle and shenanigans that played out in the Texas legislature. I knew politicians who used other people's money to build their own political base or get rich through favored deals. I also had been skeptical enough to know that excess flattery or a few campaign bucks thrown Ann's way by a few conservative high rollers came because we probably had something large—or small—that they wanted from the governor's office. They were usually happy to accept invitations to some prestigious function in the Governor's Mansion. But when their financial interests were on the line, there was no question where their support would be on election day. Many of the wealthy Texans we had cultivated, entertained, and welcomed into Ann's administration ended up backing Bush in the 1994 campaign. But a few powerful people were not enamored with the possibility of a Bush holding the governor's office and stuck with Ann during the hard times.

Another Kind of Celebrity

During the last few weeks of the reelection campaign, a very different kind of celebrity came into my life—a famous man who probably had a greater fortune than Richard Rainwater. Former third-party presidential candidate Ross Perot endorsed Ann and gave her $50,000, not an insignificant contribution at the time even in Texas politics. There were no strings attached—Perot didn't want anything from Ann. He simply didn't like the Bushes, based on his 1992 presidential campaign experiences against George Herbert Walker Bush and Bill Clinton.

Although the national news media had ridiculed Perot's quirky personality, he had a stellar reputation in Texas not only as a visionary business leader but also as a serious advocate for quality public education. His family supported the arts, medical research, and even Planned Parenthood. We were thrilled with his late endorsement, hoping it would shore up Ann's declining support in the business community.

In the final weeks of the campaign, Perot started calling me at home at night to make sure I was running the campaign up to his high standards. Did I know what was going on in the field? Was I personally talking to voters, instead of relying solely on professional pollsters? What was Ann saying on the stump? What could we, or should we, be doing that we were not? All good questions, of course, and I did my best to give him thoughtful and honest answers. To my surprise, I really came to like the old man. He knew how to get things done and was trying to help our flagging campaign. But I was usually dead tired at the end of the day and came to dread those nightly calls. I already knew that our campaign was on a downward spiral. Perot's reminders of our inadequacies were not what I wanted to hear. Unfortunately, even with Ross Perot's good advice, our campaign limped to the finish line without the edge or good luck we had hoped for.

Experiences like these with Ross Perot, Perry Bass, and indirectly Richard Rainwater gave me a lot to think about in relation to the political life I so loved. When I retreated back into teaching again, I had the opportunity, time, and isolation to do so.

In Defense of Politics

When I taught at the LBJ School of Public Affairs, I always assigned my students Bernard Crick's great book on the meaning and uses of politics, *In Defense of Politics*. Crick was a British scholar who described what he believed to be the essence of authentic politics. He defined politics in a democratic system as an *activity*, not an ideology. For Crick, politics was a set of actions designed to preserve a community grown too complicated for either tradition alone or pure arbitrary rule to preserve it without the undue use of coercion.[4]

We most often think of politics as the art of winning elections. However, authentic politics in a thriving democracy goes deeper, according to Crick. It is a relational process to determine how and with whom we govern ourselves. At its best it might provide a way for differing interests to be accommodated and conciliated by giving them a share in power in proportion to their importance to the welfare and survival of the whole community. The key words for Crick were conciliation and share. His deeper view of politics transcended the kinds of internecine backroom warfare or rivalry that goes on within political campaigns or the more cynical Machiavellian practice of manipulation that we've come to associate with inflated hate-filled rhetoric or dubious tactical behavior in legislative maneuvers. That kind of behavior may be attributed more to the vagaries of human nature than solely to some inherent nature of politics. After all, we see the same type of manipulative, deceptive behavior in business, the professions, academia, and even organized religion. But in terms of choosing how we are governed, according to Crick, politics in its most idealistic and authentic iteration should provide public space for actions by ordinary people who want to improve their lives.

Political philosopher Hannah Arendt frequently wrote about the joy of public life for free people—the pleasure of participating in discussions, deliberations, and decisions about various courses of action without fear of reprisal. Those activities represent politics in its very best iteration. We see it most often in local communities, where people can clearly recognize their common interests despite their different backgrounds or opinions.

From my earliest days in San Antonio to my most recent ventures, I have loved being in discussions and deliberations with people who talked about ideas or issues and who cared about the core values that mattered: fairness and equality, liberty and justice. Maybe that was as much a part of my compulsion to be involved in Texas politics as were the adrenaline rushes of campaigns or the excitement of hobnobbing with celebrities. But those discussions also taught me that we are much more effective when we operate in the "world as it is," instead of the "world as it should be."[5] Magical thinking does not provoke change.

Politics is often chaotic, as sometimes reflected in the messy desk of those involved in a campaign, like my desk in Governor Ann Richards's unsuccessful reelection campaign in 1994.

If we are stuck in some sort of ideology or a rigid set of beliefs that promises a perfect world and requires our purity over practical actions, then we are limiting our effectiveness in the public arena. Ideology offers a distorted version of the world—whether it is driven by religious dogma, Marxist theory, an idealized vision of a free market, a libertarian Ayn Rand view of life, or the purity politics of the anarchist Left. Ideology rarely fits the reality of the moment. And it has little value in figuring out the practicalities of actually winning an election or governing a city or state.

To be effective in the politics of governing, we have to learn to live with the tension between the perfect solution to our problems and the one that just may be "good enough." That's when we most often have to bargain, deal, or settle for something less than ideal in order to get part of what we believe is necessary. And yet, when all the doors are closed to us, with no openings for real bargaining to deal with issues of fairness and justice, other tactics are often necessary to force accountability for those who hold total power. That's when we see protests, confrontations, lawsuits, marches, demonstrations, sit-ins, civil disobedience, or provocations. It was the combination of these tactics that allowed the civil rights movement, the woman suffrage movement, and even the early labor movement to prevail. Contrary to conservative conventional wisdom, these tactics actually fall into the realm of authentic politics as long as they are nonviolent. When they are prohibited or repressed by authoritarian leaders who are threatened by authentic political action, we see the failure of politics. All hell can break loose, and fear and violence can take hold.

It took me a long time to understand that reality. And I had to go far away to confront it.

Poland

Poland?

Yes. It was in Poland that I got a taste of what the failure of politics might be like.

I spent a month there one summer working with students at the National Institute for Public Administration.

Shortly after the success of the Solidarity movement, the breakup of the Soviet Union, and the fall of the Communist government in Poland, the new democratic government established a graduate-level program to train the next generation of civil servants who had not been part of the Soviet-era nomenklatura or steeped in the old authoritarian culture.

The summer program with visiting scholars was developed by the institute in partnership with the LBJ School of Public Affairs at the University of Texas at Austin, and I volunteered to be part of the new venture.

Little did I know at the time that I would find so many of the truths that I had struggled to understand when I went exploring in the deep well of Texas politics. They were all there in Poland.

WHEN MY ILLUSTRIOUS TEACHING COLLEAGUE and former member of Congress Barbara Jordan found out I was going to Poland, she jokingly asked if I was being punished for some misdeed at the LBJ School. After all, Poland was one of the most backward of the major Eastern European countries and one of the last to throw off the yoke of Russian oppression. However, Eleanor and I had actually visited Billy in Russia the previous summer, when he was editing an ex-pat weekly magazine covering the political and cultural changes spreading over the old Soviet Union. The fledgling democracy movement was emerging in Russia, and Boris Yeltsin had become the first president of the

New Russian Federation. I was particularly eager to compare what was happening in Poland to what we had experienced in Russia.

I prepared for my visit to Poland by reading *The Captive Mind* and other works by the Nobel Prize poet Czeslaw Milosz as well as the writings of Solidarity leader Adam Michnik, then editor of Warsaw's largest newspaper, *Gazeta Wyborcza*. Yet, nothing really prepared me for what I would experience.

Americans were everywhere. Economic experts from the United States Agency for International Development (USAID) were searching for projects to fund. US businesses were invading the country with big ideas to create a capitalist economy. I even connected with an old political friend from Austin, Alan Hirst, who was then the head of Citibank in Poland. Another friend from Texas, Susan Snell, was in Poland as a Peace Corps volunteer. Her mission was to identify potential tourist sites so the new government could attract foreign visitors and their much-needed dollars. New shops and restaurants were opening everywhere. But the old Poland was very much in evidence too. My students at the institute were caught in a whirlwind of change. And it was not easy to adjust.

Almost two dozen young men and women in their twenties and thirties had been assigned to my lectures at the institute in a nondescript building in Warsaw's city center. While most students could understand and speak English, a young translator attended my sessions to help over any rough spots. I was excited to be part of this new teaching opportunity but was soon puzzled and troubled by the classroom environment. In the heady days after the fall of communism, many of these young men and women were still locked in their internal struggles between hope and cynicism and seemed disdainful of so-called foreign experts like me. During my first two class sessions, they continued to talk among themselves and ignore my lecture. I was clearly not connecting with them, so I asked my young translator if something was wrong with my lecture—or me. He advised me not to take the class behavior personally and tried to reassure me about my presence at the institute. In the old system, classroom rudeness was one of the few ways students could thumb their noses at the authoritarian babble of Soviet lackeys. As he explained, "Old habits are dying hard in the new Poland."

With this new information, the only thing I knew to do was throw out my carefully prepared notes and start over to see if I could find some sort of common ground to connect with these bright young men and women. So I told them a little about myself and my life in Texas politics as an outsider who ultimately became an insider. I asked them if there might be anything in my experiences in politics or government that might be useful to them in their new positions. My nervous self-revelations stimulated their curiosity. It was a new educational experience of openness for them—and for me—and they responded enthusiastically with earnest questions that were pretty basic to anyone who has to operate within a bureaucracy.

They wanted to learn how to deal with the stupidity and rigidity of administrators who refused to adapt to the new wave of openness. They wanted to know what to do with incompetent employees who simply couldn't be fired because they had powerful connections. They needed ideas for dealing with a wave of corruption that the new market freedoms were facilitating. They were trying to understand how to operate in harmony with the sudden release of long-suppressed individualism, which was becoming an impediment to serious institutional change. Mostly, they seemed to really want to learn how to develop a new way of political life that would be totally different from the authoritarian regimes of the past. Of course, I didn't have ready answers for their questions, but they did indicate the difficulty of making the changes they were undertaking.

As I got to know the students on a personal basis, visiting their homes and sharing meals with them, I began to understand the fragility of the emerging democracy movement that they and many of the leaders of the Solidarity movement were trying to build. Their early euphoria was already being dampened by reality.

One of the young men I met was particularly worried about an already perceived drift back into authoritarianism. He was originally from Kielce, an industrial town of about 200,000 about halfway between Warsaw and Krakow. He knew that his city had not yet emerged into the modern era and perhaps had not escaped its anti-Semitic past. The city is believed to be the site of the last anti-Jewish pogrom in Europe *after* the end of World War II. Yet he was one of the few Poles I met who was willing to talk about Poland's anti-Semitic past and problematic future. A free thinker, he feared a return to a form of Catholic absolutism that controlled every aspect of personal life, even before the Nazi and Communist takeovers. And he was fearful that Solidarity's charismatic leader, Lech Walesa, might not be strong enough to resist the old authoritarian forces that seemed to be emerging again. The age-old conflict between modernity and religion, freedom and authority, seemed to be playing out within the new Polish democracy.

Nowhere was the contrast between the old and new Poland more evident than in my visit to Czestochowa to see the famous icon of the Black Madonna at Jasna Gora Cathedral.

It was there on the grassy grounds surrounding the fourteenth-century monastery that Pope John Paul II, the former Polish priest who had supported the Solidarity movement, came to hold his first Mass in Poland after the fall of communism. Every Sunday pilgrims from all over Poland came there to pay tribute to the icon of the cherished Black Madonna. The Virgin, whose bejeweled image was captured in a dark four-foot-high wooden icon, had been crowned the Queen and Protector of Poland for the "miracle" of saving the monastery from foreign invaders three centuries ago. But while the blessed Madonna was credited with saving the monastery, she had not been able to help the Jews and even devout Catholics who perished at Auschwitz, only a short distance away. It was there that my understanding of the failure of politics and reality of absolute power crystallized.

The Camps

The LBJ School of Public Affairs had sent not only teachers like me to Poland that summer but also three bright, optimistic graduate students who were studying at Jagiellonian University in Krakow, one of Eastern Europe's oldest centers of learning. Mark Vane, Jenny Jordan, Scott Sheppard, and I were able to visit Auschwitz together, along with my friends Margaret Keys and James Elrod, who happened to be in Poland at the time.

We walked into the camp through the gates over rail tracks that had carried hundreds of thousands of Jews, Gypsies, Poles, homosexuals, and others to their deaths. From the time I entered that space, it was like I was on another plane of existence: heavy, surreal, and so removed from my grasp of reality that I felt instantly lost to myself. It was a place filled with the smell of death without any discernible odor. The failure of German politics and turn to Adolf Hitler's brutal, demonic anti-Semitism in the 1930s had led directly to this.

While we were in the camp, a German church group lit candles at the "execution" wall and sang hymns that only heightened the surreal nature of the experience.

We saw the ovens. We stood in a gas chamber. My breath was taken away, first when I saw two tons of human hair shaved from the heads of female victims and later when I saw the collection of shoes taken from infants and children. I felt like I had come face to face with the pure power of evil.

More than a million men, women, and children had been killed at Auschwitz. Their ashes from the crematoriums had blown over the fields of Birkenau, now part of the memorial to the dead. As we walked on those sacred fields, the scale of the land and the sight of the decaying wooden structures in the distance that housed the gas chambers and ovens stoked the horror I felt. On the wall of a little museum in the field was a letter from a girl who beseeched her mother to "look for me among the ashes in the fields at Birkenau." I came away from our day in Birkenau and Auschwitz with something deeper than sorrow—pure emptiness of being.

Back in my hotel room later that day in beautiful Krakow, I tried to come to grips emotionally with the fact that 60,000 Jews had lived in Krakow at the start of the war. There were 150 at the end. Where did they go? Were they in the fields of Birkenau where I had so recently strolled? What did the inhabitants of the beautiful old city of Krakow know of this? And what, if anything, did they do about it? Is it possible to live so close to constant death—to the agony and torture—and not know, not feel, the energy of evil? Never to see it coming?

Shoah, Claude Lanzmann's compelling 1985 eleven-hour documentary about German Holocaust sites across Poland, asked the same question again and again, probing to learn whether ordinary Poles knew what was going on. Many of those he interviewed admitted that they did know but tried to look away to avoid any "unpleasantness." One engineer who drove the trains into the camps said that he could hear the cries of those in the railcars behind his locomotive. The German guards on the train gave vodka to him and other workers on their runs, and he was never allowed to look inside at his human cargo. Otherwise, he said, he couldn't have done it.[1]

After watching, or rather experiencing, Lanzmann's *Shoah*, the late film critic Roger Ebert felt that the Holocaust is "no longer a subject, a chapter of history, a phenomenon. It is an environment. It is around us."[2] He was shocked at the revelation that ordinary people speaking in ordinary voices of the time could participate in the killing of other ordinary people.

Poland is still haunted by Auschwitz and its past complicity with anti-Semitism.

The right-of-center ruling Law and Justice Party passed a law in 2018 making it illegal for Poles to attribute any responsibility for Nazi crimes committed by the German Third Reich to the Polish nation. Any Polish citizen who speaks about Poland's co-responsibility for the Holocaust could spend three years in prison. This hard-core denial of any form of Polish complicity in the Holocaust came after new research revealed numerous massacres of Jews in Poland *before* the German-Russian occupation began in 1939. There had also been widespread blackmailing of Jews by their Polish neighbors, and an auxiliary police force made up of mostly prewar Polish policemen was thought to be responsible for tens of thousands of deaths.[3] Poles did not want to acknowledge this ancient, endemic anti-Semitism and certainly didn't want to talk about it. Most importantly, the increasingly authoritarian government had begun shutting down its independent judiciary system, repressing dissent, and clamping down on basic democratic institutions, even turning away from the democratic values of the old Solidarity movement, much to the consternation of its former leaders, Lech Walesa and Adam Michnik.[4]

My experiences in Poland so many years ago had made me an avid consumer of Polish news. I have tried to stay on top of all that was leading the nation away from its democratic hopes into its new totalitarian ventures, which seemed to be supported by both the educated elites and ordinary working people. Why was this happening? What were the underlying tensions that could cause a free people to make such a dramatic shift from democratic to authoritarian rule? Was this an individual or purely collective phenomenon? Was it a power grab by a scheming few or a willing acquiescence by the many? Or was it simply a force of habit from an authoritarian past? What is there in the human spirit that draws many of us—not just the good citizens of Poland—to autocratic ventures, conspiracy theories, and cultish leaders who might ultimately do harm?

The Adversary Principle

Karlfried Graf Dürckheim, a German philosopher, Jung scholar, Zen master, and Christian mystic, believed that in a quest for goodness, or in the context of welcoming others into the democratic benefits of our larger society, we always have within us what could be called a force against life.[5] Dürckheim called this force the "adversary principle." Others may call it our "shadow" or even our "demon" nature. The idea is that a link with evil always lurks in the collective unconscious and is manifest on both personal and political levels. On a personal level, it appears when we get close to true self-knowledge, answering a call to service or making a commitment to a new path of existence that might require actions that would take us out of our "comfort zone." But Dürckheim notes that this adversary principle also pops up on a societal level, when a whole nation faces massive changes that challenge some degree of perceived privilege and require a new way of being or acting in the world. Both as an individual and collective phenomenon, it seems to be rooted in a fear of loss for which others—outsiders—can be blamed. Dürckheim implies that an inner mechanism that is both personal and collective shuts off consciousness, empathy, and feeling when perceived reality is so disturbing. When there appears to be an appealing alternative interpretation that masks reality, it takes courage to resist a wave of conformity imposed by our friends or our leaders.

Some three decades after the fall of authoritarian communism in Poland and earnest, hopeful experiments with democracy, a new kind of collective adversary power seemed to have emerged to halt the nation's progress. As late as 2020, political dissidents, critical journalists, and even rock stars have been censored or thrown into jail for questioning the accumulation of power by an increasingly authoritarian government. My young friend from Kielce was surprisingly prophetic.

There are few simple answers to explain why it is so threatening to so many people to see a new future that reshapes the face of power and expands the field of those who may hold it. Maybe, as Anne Applebaum suggests in her book *Twilight of Democracy: The Seductive Lure of Authoritarianism*, it is the fear of complexity that leads a diverse democracy to flee from its most cherished ideals. Maybe it is a "frame of mind, not a set of ideas." It seems to be tied to some sort of bitter resentment that attracts such fervent followers to problematic leaders who appear to have simple answers to complex issues and know how to inflame old grievances.[6]

Poland, Power, and Pontification

What do Poland, the camps, and the adversary principle have to do with my time in the deep well of Texas politics? Why do I even bring them up now when I ponder my illusions and delusions in this set of reflections that cover some of the events in my life?

Part of the answer, I believe, is that I'm still sorting out the conflicting messages that emerge when our successes somehow turn so easily to failure. I saw that in Poland and experienced that in Texas. I think it all ultimately comes back to power—how you get it, how you use it, and how you can sustain it.

Liberals like me, who find ourselves with a modicum of power when we operate at higher levels of government, have to remind ourselves how quickly our successes can be reversed. We often have to fight the same battles over and over again. That means that we have to make the best and wisest uses of power when we are fortunate enough to hold it and have to become comfortable using the power we actually hold.

By the time I became Ann Richards's chief of staff, I had already come to believe the fundamental truth, once expressed by Nelson Mandela, that those who wanted to "wipe poverty off the face of the earth must use . . . weapons other than kindness."[7] But kindness should never be mistaken for weakness. Fortunately, the arsenal of democratic politics contains numerous weapons available to public officials to begin wiping poverty off the face of the earth. Pompous pontifications from old liberals like me may be one of those weaker weapons, but they can sometimes serve a useful purpose on their own.

Thousands of stories in the long tale of human history arise from heroic efforts to redress the unfair conditions of life brought on by dangerous concentrations of power. All authentic political battles are struggles to deal with this dangerous imbalance in order to achieve some ideal public "good." And this is where my old idealism gets stuck. For me, the good means that all people should have opportunities for work, income, education, safety, and health. But equally important to me is the belief that people are free only when they are allowed to live in dignity, avoid humiliation, and be assured of enough justice to experience some fairness in their life and circumstances.

The Bottom of the Well?

I think I always intuitively understood that holding political power in Texas would never be easy. But it would be the only way to bring about the changes we believed were necessary to achieve some notion of public good. *That's what the whole damn thing was about!* And I was completely comfortable with using the minuscule level of power we actually held. Theologian Reinhold Niebuhr's exploration of Christian realism resonated with me, particularly his admonition for liberals, who considered themselves to be the "children of light," to become as wily as the "children of darkness," who are guided only by their own self-interest.

"The preservation of a democratic civilization requires the wisdom of the serpent and the harmlessness of the dove," he wrote. "The children of light must be armed with the wisdom of the children of darkness but remain free from their malice. They must know the power of self-interest in human society without giving it moral justification." I learned from Niebuhr that liberals had to develop this kind of wisdom to "beguile, deflect, harness, and restrain self-interest, individual and collective, for the sake of the community."[8] Texas liberals, including me, were just not very good at figuring out how to put Niebuhr's advice into action.

I actually sought this kind of wily wisdom, but it did not come easily. My hope had been to achieve some sort of balance in the distribution of power, knowing that it often required compromise and conciliation in a manner that might actually improve human life. But that kind of relational power is always tenuous. And it requires continuous, focused effort to sustain it. *That is one of the hard truths I found at the bottom of my well.*

I value my experiences in the world of Texas politics, and over time I came to terms with its unique rawness. My addiction or compulsion to participate in politics added no small amount of spice and, yes, excitement to my life. For so much of that time, there was real joy in the midst of the craziness and competition. In the best of the Ann Richards days, we were part of a community trying to do the "right thing." I believe that most of us felt in a deeply personal way that we were actually serving the good, even when we lost so many battles along the way. I don't think this was simply one of those romantic illusions that I carried throughout my life. Rather, I believe that it may be another one of those "truths" that I have struggled to understand.

Maybe the best that we can do when we are facing our political losses, as Carl Jung has said, is to walk forward "step by next intuitively right step until one day, pausing to catch our breath, we turn around and gasp at a path that is still true for us."[9] Or, whenever we no longer have the power to act, maybe we should just remember what John Rogers always said: "We don't have time to get discouraged. We just have to keep yelling."

If, in my old age, yelling can only be expressed in my writings, and in occasional pontifications, then so be it!

Words

The human need to tell our stories unfolds in so many different forms: cave paintings, songs, letters, journals, history, fiction, poetry, biography, commentary, memoir, and God only knows what other forms spill from that need.

The great Czech novelist Milan Kundera believed that one reason so many of us want to write is because everyone has trouble accepting the fact that we will disappear, unheard of and unnoticed in an indifferent universe. We all want to create our own universe of words before it's too late.

Prolific writer Anne Lamott believes that the thrill of seeing oneself in print provides some sort of primal verification that we exist in the eyes of others. Because we are imagining creatures, some of us are driven to conjure stories to explain ourselves, perhaps to justify our experiences within the context of a larger history.

Zadie Smith says that writing for her is simply a psychological quirk, "developed in response to whatever personal failings I have. . . . There is no great difference between novels and banana bread. They are both just something to do."

My urge to write, to put words together, is mainly to figure out what I think and feel and what I hope others might think or feel. But as I get older I realize that it is also "just something to do."

Still, it helps to keep it all in perspective.

Once, when one of my old Sicilian aunts was telling me about a distant cousin, she said, "You know, she's just like you . . . she types." And maybe that is exactly what people like me do—type out words and hope they make sense, if not to others, at least to ourselves. We mull and meander around in our own inner world, trying to understand who we are, what we have done, and if any of it matters to anyone other than our imagining self.

MY MOTHER GAVE ME A subscription to the *Texas Observer* when I was a 17-year-old freshman at the University of Texas. Of the 25,000 students then at the university, I was probably the only freshman who had been given such a send-off, with words and ideas contained in the liberal *Texas Observer*. But then, it was a completely normal act for my mother, La Americana.

She had been a subscriber to the *Observer* from its inception in 1954, when wealthy Houstonian Frankie Randolph wanted to create a state-wide publication that covered issues and people ignored by the state's major newspapers. Randolph persuaded young Ronnie Dugger to take the helm. He produced a fiercely independent muckraking paper that became the bible for Texas liberals, highlighting in depth all the issues that mattered to working folks and Texas's minority populations. As my mother's daughter, I grew up on Ronnie Dugger's rich, evocative words about Texas politics.

Becoming a Reader

My mother made me a reader—not by coercion or force but by the lure of her companionship. She read for escape, for information, and for knowledge of a world she could never hope to enter. When she was still in her twenties with four little girls under ten, she would make a fresh pot of coffee every afternoon and sit down at our kitchen table to read. I sat with her at first not to read but simply to be with her. As the oldest child, I rarely had her full attention because she was so busy with the younger ones. But those afternoons became our quiet time together within the hectic craziness of her days. I knew my mother savored my affection, and she often encouraged me to sit alongside her and read as well. It was during those afternoons that I became a reader like my mother as well as a confirmed coffee drinker before I was ten years old.

Anita Hicks Coniglio was a beautiful woman who also had a fertile mind and a deep intellectual curiosity. The façade of personal beauty and the pursuit of learning were equally important to her. One day she came into my third-grade class to drop off the lunch box I had forgotten that morning. She wore a dark green wool fitted coat, with tiny covered buttons down the front, and she had on a small leopard-skin hat that matched the little fur pouch she loved to carry. She looked so glamorous that kids wanted to know, "Who's that?" I was so proud to tell my classmates that she was my mother. Later, as the hat and fur pouch fell out of fashion, Martha and I played dress-up with them. They became a staple in the toy box for our younger sisters, Benita and Susie.

After we moved into a larger house in the 1950s and my little sisters were in school, Anita got involved in the PTA, the Democratic Party, and the United Nations Association. One of her fellow PTA members called her a Communist because of her volunteer work with the UN. But that was Dallas in the 1950s during the McCarthy Red Scare: anyone who supported an international organization, the national Democratic Party, or even the Methodist church was considered "suspicious." One local attorney who would later be elected to the Texas state Senate claimed that the Methodist church was full of Communists because of its adherence to the Social Gospel that put an emphasis on help and justice for the poorest among us. My Methodist mother met every right-wing criterion for subversive danger. But none of that stopped her from doing what she believed was right. She even took me out of school one day to go with her to hear Eleanor Roosevelt speak at a luncheon to benefit the UN. My mother did more than support good causes, however. She provided a haven of support for all of our teenage friends whenever they needed encouragement.

At my twentieth high school class reunion, one of my friends who had lived in our neighborhood when we were kids told me, "I always loved your mother. She was the first one who told me what 'fuck' meant." When I told my then 70-year-old mother what my friend had said, she was shocked. "Oh, I couldn't have done that," she protested. "I could never say that word, especially then." But she added with a smile, "I may have told her what 'intercourse' meant." And I'm sure that's what she actually did. Words mattered to her.

Anita loved flowers, had a green thumb, knew the names of shrubs and trees, and did all of the yard work at our new house. She belonged to a neighborhood garden club that paid me five dollars one summer to paint a purple iris on the covers of its little membership directories. But painting flowers did not interest me. Words did. My mother's gift was to let me know that writers could put words together to enrich individual lives and change the world—or maybe even the state of Texas.

I think that many voracious readers at some point express a desire to write. Maybe that is how it started with me. I remember writing a little play that my fifth-grade class performed. When I transferred to a new elementary school in the seventh grade, I helped write the lyrics for our new school song. I was nerdy enough to like writing term papers in high school. My senior paper was an analysis of Fyodor Dostoevsky's *Crime and Punishment*—a vast overreach of my zeal and skills. But I had an English teacher who made our class members write for ten minutes at the beginning of each day. Maybe it was only an exercise to describe a rose in a vase on her desk or the sounds we heard from outside the open window. But it was "writing." Most of the kids hated those projects, but I loved them.

I had become a prodigious reader and aspiring writer. By the time I got to college, however, it was journalism that interested me, not writing literary fiction or poetry. I was already a news hound, and my curiosity about what was happening in the world was insatiable. I have never regretted that choice because it led to John, our children, and a common love of politics. Still, writing in one form or another became a daily part of my life.

Although I never worked for a newspaper as a reporter or editor, I did take on occasional freelance writing assignments. And I was lucky that every job I ever had involved writing in some form or another. I had numerous opportunities to think about words and their meanings. But I obviously came to prefer the quick rewards of more lively, people-centered, on-the-ground political campaigns to some sort of solitary pursuit of the serious craft of writing. Yet for many years I vacillated—writing or doing? I kept choosing "doing" until life's circumstances intervened.

Cold Anger

It was during John's four-year cancer ordeal in the 1980s that I pulled inward and began thinking more seriously about long-form writing. I rose early every morning to gaze at the sky and into the valley below our hilltop home and began playing with words to describe the rush of feelings and events that we were experiencing. We were caught in a powerful undertow of cancer and its aftermath, and daily writing became my coping mechanism. I also desperately wanted to try something different, but politics was all I knew.

A writer friend who had shed the religious rigidity of his Nazarene preacher father suggested that I write about how people brought their religious values into politics. We had often talked about the confluence of politics and religion. He was increasingly disturbed by the growing influence of Jerry Falwell's Moral Majority, the political organizing of Ralph Reed, and the rightward pull of zealous evangelicals on Southern politicians—particularly in Texas. Our conversations forced me to reexamine my own spiritual curiosity. I was instinctively drawn to the religious-based community organizing of Ernesto Cortes rather than the growing cadre of right-wing operatives whose rigidity and narrow interpretation of Christianity was so different from my own.

I had known Ernie Cortes from my San Antonio days when he was one of those young students that Albert Peña mentored. I had read about what he was now doing in San Antonio. Although I didn't know if he would remember me, I called him. He did remember—but most particularly he remembered John. He invited me to attend some of his meetings and events. I watched Cortes conduct training sessions for organizers and leaders, people he discovered in parishes and churches who had extensive relationships with others and exhibited potential for leadership. I began interviewing these men and women, whose lives were being transformed as they began to understand foundational issues that kept their neighborhoods poor and underserved by San Antonio's city government, while the North Side Anglo communities flourished.

Cortes's community leaders were developing the skills to confront those who held power in the city and to challenge them with their election-day votes. I could see that his organization, COPS (Communities Organized for Public Service), was beginning to bring about the kinds of political and policy changes that the old Democratic Coalition in San Antonio had tried to achieve when John and I were involved in the 1960s. But this was different. And I was particularly drawn to the religious underpinnings of all that Cortes was doing. Confrontations and community actions were centered in what Catholic bishops had called the preferential option for the poor.

As political or confrontational as these efforts might be, what struck me most was that the organizations never folded or went away after either victory or defeat. They were sustainable, largely because Cortes's efforts involved developing natural leaders whose deeper values were rooted in the teachings of their parishes and churches as well as fundamental democratic principles of self-government. They were practicing what I had come to consider an "authentic" politics. They were in it for the long haul, which had rarely been the case in many of the campaign-oriented political organizations that supported my causes and candidates. Although they, like all disaffected people, seethed at the injustices and discrimination they faced almost daily, Cortes was teaching them to turn their hot anger down a notch or two and transform it into what he called "cold anger," a strong, focused tool of action that used anger's energy, but not its fury, to bring about change.

A book began to take shape in my mind, and I summoned the time and energy to work on it. Because of John's cancer diagnosis in 1983, I had significantly pulled back from my extraneous involvement in Austin politics. I went to my office each day at the State Treasury and did what was necessary to help oversee the staff that Ann Richards had assembled to direct the agency's increasingly sophisticated money management efforts. But I no longer rushed off to meetings after work or on weekends. Our children were in college and on their way to independent lives, so I was relatively free to spend time with John and to think about how to actually write a book. John encouraged me to take on the project and even bought me our first computer—essentially a simple word-processing device that made the actual mechanics of writing easier and speedier than my old IBM Selectric typewriter. I think he was also eager to diminish my anxious, full-time hovering over him, hoping that I could leave him in peace to heal on his own terms if I became engaged in something else. So it was full steam ahead for me.

To understand the underlying work of Cortes, I began reading about liberation theology and other philosophical and biblical underpinnings of his efforts. He gave me books and articles, and I plunged deeper into topics of justice, power, economic equality, institutional democracy, and other subjects that I had never seriously explored. I read theologians and philosophers like Walter Brueggemann, Leonardo Boff, Gustavo Gutiérrez, Hans Küng, Paulo Freire, Reinhold Niebuhr, Hannah Arendt, and others. During that time, I became friends with several nuns, who had become community organizers within the various Industrial Areas Foundation (IAF) organizations. They were particularly interesting to me because they carried the vows of their religious orders into political life. Sister Christine Stephens and Sister Pearl Ceasar, who were members of the Congregation of Divine Providence Order in San Antonio, influenced my thinking about the challenge of combining action and contemplation to achieve political goals. Later, when I was Ann Richards's chief of staff, Sister Christine did not hesitate to call me out if I did not meet her high standards of service and accountability.[2]

As I began writing about what I was seeing on my regular trips to San Antonio, my dear friend Betty Sue Flowers helped me shape what I was learning into stories—not explanatory passages. Betty Sue was a poet, an English professor at the University of Texas, and had worked with Bill Moyers and Joseph Campbell on the PBS series *Joseph Campbell and the Power of Myth* as well as many other Moyers productions.[3] During my research and writing, Betty Sue Flowers and Ernie Cortes became my teachers and lifelong friends, each in her or his own way deepening my understanding of the power of words to transform politics and personal lives.

John's death in 1987 interrupted my research and writing about Ernie Cortes and his work. It would be almost a year later that I was sufficiently restored to pick up the thread. The manuscript was finally off to the publisher by the time I plunged into the 1990 campaign to help Ann Richards become governor. *Cold Anger: A Story of Faith and Power Politics* was finally published shortly after Ann's November election, with a foreword by Bill Moyers.[4] Four years later, I would learn that Karl Rove had instructed George W. Bush's gubernatorial campaign staff to read my book. Because I was running Ann's reelection campaign against challenger Bush, I was told that they wanted to learn something about my "psychology" to gain insight into our campaign. Rove certainly did his research. I don't know what he found that might have been helpful to the kind of campaign he ran, but losing that race opened another door for me to write again.

Barbara Jordan: American Hero

After Barbara Jordan's death in January 1996 when she was only fifty-nine years old, writer Jan Jarboe suggested to literary agent Jim Hornfischer that I might be interested in writing a biography about Jordan. After all, Jordan and I had both been on the faculty at the LBJ School of Public Affairs, which Jan and Jim thought might give me some special insight into her illustrious career. I had actually gotten to know Jordan when Ann Richards ran for governor in 1990. She had served as co-chair of Ann's campaign and later as the unpaid ethics counsel to her administration. We always asked Jordan to interview people that Ann was considering for major appointments to judicial positions or state agency leadership roles. If Barbara Jordan questioned their character or ethics, we quickly dropped them from consideration.

Later, when I began teaching at the LBJ School, Jordan welcomed me with open arms. I was a "practitioner" instead of an academic, and practitioners were not exactly welcomed by the school's prestigious array of published scholars with PhDs. I was shocked to learn that some of the professors hadn't even welcomed the illustrious Barbara Jordan, who gave up her congressional seat in 1978 to return to Texas. Jordan's widely acclaimed testimony at the Watergate hearings and groundbreaking keynote address to the 1976 Democratic National

Convention were not quite enough to satisfy some of the school's academics. Because she had a sense of what I might be facing in my new position, she was incredibly kind to me when I arrived. I was never part of Jordan's inner circle of friends, which was small and fiercely loyal, but she did invite me to her home for several of her Friday night pizza gatherings.

Still, I thought long and hard before deciding whether I could write about Barbara Jordan. I was white, she was Black, and our experiences in the world of politics were strikingly different. I also knew how secretive Jordan had been about her private life. There were rumors that she was gay, but during her life and even after her death Jordan's closest friends were too discreet to either confirm or deny the nature of her long-term relationship with Nancy Earl. They shared a spacious home along Onion Creek, south of Austin. It was more relevant to me at the time that she never revealed the reasons she had been confined to a wheelchair shortly after she left Congress. Her illness was not disclosed until shortly after her death, when her physician revealed that she had been diagnosed with multiple sclerosis (MS) while she was still a member of Congress. That fact in particular drew me into her story almost more than anything else. I had watched my beautiful younger sister Benita become one of the victims of this terrible, progressive neurological disease, for which there is no cure. Diagnosed in her twenties shortly after she had given birth to twin boys, my sister had struggled her whole life with a remitting, relapsing form of the disease, leaving her further debilitated after each attack. And she, too, was confined to a wheelchair until she died from complications of MS in 2009. Because of my sister's struggles, I had a sense of what the illustrious Barbara Jordan might have experienced and kept so well hidden from others.

I devoted the next two years of my life to writing about this remarkable woman as well as teaching my classes at the LBJ School. Even though I discovered that serious research and writing could be a lonely process for a single person like me, the effort was taking me in new directions that were profoundly rewarding.

Although support for civil rights had always been part of my political DNA, like a lot of white professionals I really did not have a full grasp of Black history. My research for the Jordan biography plunged me headlong into discovering the reality of the Black experience after slavery in the South, which was a deadly mix of violence, fear, and legal discrimination. I also learned about the rich culture of church, family, and community that nurtured and sustained dispossessed African Americans, whose daily lives were spent trying to cope with an overwhelming infrastructure of oppression that included denial of educational and job opportunities as well as access to adequate housing and healthcare. To understand what I was seeing on the ground and learning from interviews with people who knew Barbara Jordan when she was growing up in Houston, I delved into the writings of W.E.B. Du Bois and the sermons of Howard Thurman, the great preacher and theologian, who was chaplain at Boston University and influenced both Jordan and Martin Luther King Jr. I read the biographies of Frederick Douglass, Thurgood Marshall, Fannie Lou Hamer, and others. I read the novels of Toni Morrison. I spent hours in the Houston Public Library, which had a marvelous archive containing articles and memorabilia that reflected Black life in Houston after the Civil War. John Egerton's writings about the generation of African Americans in the South before the civil rights movement helped me put Jordan's life in the context of her times and early experiences in Houston.[5]

Completing the biography of Barbara Jordan had become a pursuit that was essential to my own sense of well-being. I was writing to find out what I thought, what I felt, what I learned, and what I believed. Most importantly, writing about Barbara Jordan helped me understand my own attraction to a political life and to grasp in greater detail the trends of history that were unfolding right in front of my eyes. I had to dig, to think, to wrestle with how to express what I was seeing accurately and imaginatively. I was just a little late in beginning the serious pursuit of words that mattered. But I also discovered that curiosity had driven my motivation to write from the beginning. I had simply wanted to learn, to understand, and to know what was really going on in the world. Being able to research something that was interesting to me was a critical element in every writing project I had ever seriously undertaken. Learning something new was as important for me as the pleasure of putting words together that expressed an idea or told a story or explored an experience. My curiosity ultimately resulted in the publication of *Barbara Jordan: An American Hero* in 1998.[6]

Soon after the Jordan book was finished, I once again plunged into an intensive work environment. I loved writing, but I also needed to earn a living. That opened a brand-new chapter in my life.

PART V

New Beginnings

Change

14

KLRU-TV board chair Dr. Patricia Hayes, who at the time was president of St. Edward's University, where I had served on her board, invited me to apply for the open position to become the president and CEO of KLRU, Austin's PBS station.

But politics, as usual, intervened.

KLRU's board of directors included some of Austin's elite bankers, lawyers, and business leaders who had the financial resources to help support the station. A few were afraid that I was too much of a partisan Democrat to lead the station. Several board members grilled me repeatedly to make sure I would not destroy the station with my "left-wing" views. I was actually interviewed by seventeen members of the thirty-five-member board. After about a month of give-and-take discussions, a job offer finally came. I grabbed it. It was exciting for me to have this heady new opportunity for leadership in a brand-new venture. But I admit I had no idea of what it would actually take to handle the tasks ahead.

I WAS BOTH AMUSED AND a bit nervous when I learned that the business leaders who initially opposed me agreed to offer me the job because they thought that I might be an effective fundraiser. I shouldn't have been too surprised. In public television—as well as politics—money drives a lot of our most fundamental decisions. And there was a pressing need for new money because the station had not kept up with technology or the myriad changes underway in Austin throughout the 1980s and 1990s. So I was under pressure from my first day on the job to "fix" the station's management and fundraising structure to bring it into the digital age. I also quickly learned that my task was not only to start raising money but to schmooze with conservative board members to win their support for some of the structural changes that would make the station stronger in the Austin community.

I hit the ground running—writing foundation grant proposals, calling on potential donors, and scrambling to build a stronger membership base by focusing the station's programming more on the Austin community. Like many public television stations across the county, KLRU was almost always scrambling for funds, but the required multimillion-dollar conversion from analog to digital technology presented a new financial challenge. Unlike most PBS stations across the nation, KLRU and the twelve other public stations in Texas received no state funding for public television and had to rely heavily on private donors. So while PBS stations all across the nation were wrestling with the same digital conversion funding needs as ours, they were getting help from their state governments. Even public television stations in the traditionally conservative South—like Louisiana and Georgia—were getting supplemental grants from their state governments.

Fortunately, after being immersed in Texas politics for so long, I knew people all over the state who might have an interest in the survival of public television and might be willing to help us secure state funds to help their local stations make a smooth transition to digital technology. And I still had a few contacts in state government and among Capitol lobbyists who were willing to help us. Along with other heads of Texas's public television stations, and friends in the Texas Association of Broadcasters, we put together a coalition of community leaders to support our efforts. Because I had worked closely with Governor Rick Perry when he was still a Democrat and a member of the state legislature, we still had a cordial relationship. He allowed one of his tech-savvy staffers, Stefanie Stanford, to help us figure out how to win approval of a $13-million grant from the state's newly created Technology Infrastructure Fund. And we did. All thirteen Texas PBS stations would share the proceeds of the one-time grant—the first and only financial aid that the Lone Star state has ever given to PBS stations to date. With an additional grant from the federally funded Corporation for Public Broadcasting and growing support from Austin's philanthropic community, we were able to bring in much-needed dollars fairly soon in my tenure. Although I frequently groused about how the high-tech moguls were instrumental in promoting the rapid growth in Austin, KLRU could not have made it into the digital age without them.

Dell Computer executives were particularly important to our fundraising successes, as were some key Austin technology moguls and venture capitalists. Austin's new rich were particularly receptive to keeping our signature production, *Austin City Limits*, alive. Although it was the longest continuing running music show on American television, it was always a struggle to find the money to support its production. I was able to hire a bright young marketing executive, Ed Bailey, who got his start at the Rock and Roll Hall of Fame and Museum in Cleveland. We created a new support group—*Friends of Austin City Limits*. The group made annual contributions that provided a new source of income for the show. Still, we depended on corporate underwriting to support our enormous production costs. With the help of Kirk Watson, the mayor of Austin at the time, we were able to convince the Austin Convention Center and Tourist Bureau to help with underwriting. That entity has been a continuous supporter of the show since then.

I am especially proud that we managed to secure a stable future for the show by forging a licensing agreement with a young group of Austin concert promoters to create the *Austin City Limits* Music Festival, now one of the top two or three outdoor annual music events in the nation.[1] A rewarding side effect of raising money for *Austin City Limits* was that I got to be exposed in a deeper way to Austin's great music scene. I was thrilled to be in the production control booth with legendary producer Terry Lickona, director Gary Menotti, and their creative team for the studio tapings that would go to PBS stations all over the country. I could have never imagined that the great blues legend and fabulous guitarist Buddy Guy would leap into the audience and sit on my lap in the middle of one of his fabulous riffs during one of those tapings. That did happen, though, as well as other memorable musical events that enriched my life and my experiences at KLRU.

But KLRU was about more than music.

We had award-winning children's programming that drew young families to the station.

That became especially important on 9/11 when terrorists flew planes into New York's landmark Twin Towers at the World Trade Center. Every network and television station in the country was providing round-the-clock coverage of the unfolding tragedy that took nearly 3,000 lives in a single day. The repeated images of the explosive collapse of the Twin Towers were devastating. The national PBS program distribution service gave local stations the option of continuing with our morning children's programs to provide a safe haven for kids away from the unfolding disaster images or to take the general news feeds about the horrible events of the day. In Austin we stuck with the kids, so that thousands of children in our multicounty viewing area would not be traumatized by the horrible images. We willingly gave up our adult viewers who wanted to see the breaking news because they could tune in to any network or cable station in our area. Although I never doubted that we made the right decision, it was still gratifying over the next few weeks to get thank-you notes from grateful parents who felt that we helped them protect their children during those awful hours and days.

Immediately after 9/11, we devoted one of our now-frequent televised town-hall meetings to address the fears and concerns of young people. We brought in religious leaders of all faiths as well as public safety officials to answer the questions and meet with high-school students from our area. We stayed focused on their concerns whenever new facts emerged.

Over the years we staged other televised town-hall meetings to discuss or debate community problems on pressing issues. We brought in technology leaders to address a growing digital divide in our area. We delved into environmental topics like protections for Austin's fabulous Barton Springs natural pool, a community treasure. Because our televised studio town-hall meetings explored many other important local and national issues, we were attracting more civic-minded viewers to the station. That was an important part of our efforts to build our membership and funding base.

We even started a speakers' series that attracted world-renowned writers like Salman Rushdie, Carlos Fuentes, historians David McCullough and Doris Kearns Goodwin, and filmmakers like Spike Lee. We were able to develop a reputation for incisive, insightful public affairs programming, which was most important to me. With significant funding from my friend Jack Martin, we managed to produce a weekly interview show that drew illustrious national guests, with host Evan Smith. He was editor of *Texas Monthly* at the time and later went on to create one of the best online news sites in the nation—*Texas Tribune*. In addition, with funding from one of the *Texas Observer*'s financial angels, Bernard Rapoport, we could cover the antics of the Texas legislature in a weekly show, hosted by the award-winning documentary filmmaker Paul Stekler.

Austin was gaining a reputation within the national PBS system not only as the producer of one of its signature music programs but as a community catalyst that enhanced its overall mission to provide education, entertainment, and enlightenment as a way to build an informed citizenry.

I loved our institutionalized commitment to democratic values and enjoyed talking about it to anyone who would listen. During this time, I made dozens of speeches and received the kinds of honors awarded as much for "position" as for merit. But I was putting in eleven- or twelve-hour days, and my writings were confined to reports to the board, newsletters, and station publications. I had little time for anything else. As much as I loved being part of the PBS community both locally and nationally, it was time for another change. I felt that I had reached the limit of what I wanted or could do at KLRU. Perhaps it was time for new leadership to take it to a higher level than I had the energy to pursue. As a result, I was delighted when the board selected veteran community leader Bill Stotesbery to be my successor. I stayed on an extra month to ease the transition from the old to the new. Because Austin PBS has thrived in recent years, I obviously left the station in good hands under its new leader. Still, I am grateful that I got to be part of the grand PBS venture that serves all Americans in every area of the country.

When I decided to leave KLRU, however, I decided to leave Austin as well.

I had entered my early sixties and felt the urgency of passing time. The power of words beckoned, as did my larger family in Dallas. Intuitively I knew that the richness of my Austin days was over. Of course, I would miss my brother, Frank, nephew Anthony, and his mom Janet, who lived there. But Austin had changed. And so had I.

One of the factors leading to my decision to leave Austin was an awareness that surprises so many of us when we become grandparents. A new dimension is added to our lives. The world seems brighter, and something shifts within. When I became a grandmother, my young granddaughters Lauren and Lindsey (to whom this book is dedicated) exerted the same pull on me as had my own children. I wanted to be with them whenever I could. I had been making frequent visits to see them in Dallas whenever I could get away from KLRU over a weekend. Because of them and Eleanor and my son-in-law Mark, it was surprisingly easy in 2004 to flee the beautiful Hill Country of Central Texas and the politics and glitter of Austin, where I had lived most of my adult life. My friends thought I was crazy. They didn't understand that I had come to want more from life than political or professional success. I wanted family. I wanted simplicity. I wanted time to "just be."

Dallas

When I came to Dallas, I felt like a different woman. I bought a little mid-century house on Joe's Creek, one of the few remaining spring-fed creeks that had not been paved over in the city's massive urban and suburban development. My backyard sloped down to the creek, which drew all sorts of wildlife—beavers, ducks, hawks, and huge white egrets that waited patiently in the creek for one of their daily treats of small fish. Brazen raccoons had owned the neighborhood long before

the modest homes were built there in the 1950s, and an occasional coy-
ote or bobcat would emerge from the woods around the creek to clear
the area of squirrels—at least for a few days. It was a nature oasis in a
decidedly urban environment and a great place to play with my grandchildren and to host large family gatherings. When Billy moved to Dallas a few years later, I was lucky enough to have all of that and more.

Although we had lost both of our parents, my three younger sisters still lived in Dallas at the time, and it had been more than thirty
years since I had been able to see them on a regular basis. For the first
time since the early years of my marriage when I was minding young
children or trying to manage a busy work life, there was nothing I
had to do with any sense of urgency every single day. Although I did
take on several consulting gigs, I was unencumbered by obligations or
major responsibilities. It was a wonderful feeling. I kept tooling around
with ideas for a book. Nothing seemed to gel, but it really didn't seem
to bother me. Then I started paying attention to what was going on
around me.

Dallas was no longer the right-wing mecca that I had fled as a 17-year-
old girl looking for adventure and perhaps a career as a journalist and
writer. Something was shifting; a political change was underway. What
was going on? Texas politics seemed to be calling me again—even in my
new surroundings. I just couldn't help it.

I wanted to understand how Dallas was beginning to emerge from
the decades-long Republican domination that had helped sweep Ann
Richards from office in such a decisive way in the 1990s. By 2006 a
small group of Dallas's progressive Democrats had been able to make
inroads into key political offices in the city. They had new sources of
money and had obviously developed sufficient political moxie to win
elections for countywide offices and even pick up some legislative
seats. I could see from the data that they were being helped along by
key demographic shifts underway—this time away from solid Republican precincts to moderate, even liberal districts.

I wanted to know the new Democratic players who understood how
to capitalize on demographic trends that were emerging in the early
2000s—just as Karl Rove had spotted the countervailing trends in the

early 1990s that wiped out the Democratic establishment in Dallas and the rest of the state. I became friends with a remarkable group of smart political operatives and a group of women who were part of Annie's List, a statewide organization dedicated to electing pro-choice women to public office in Texas.[2] I was able to reconnect with other long-time Democratic leaders who had fought the lengthy battles for years and were energized by the new possibilities. Even more amazing to me was that a large group of significant new Democratic donors had emerged in Dallas by 2006. Many of them became financial "bundlers" for President Obama's 2008 and 2012 campaigns. But the added bonus to my new political interests was my Dallas "lunch bunch"—Pat Panburn, Mary Mapes, Russell Langley, Lisa Turner, and Joe Armstrong. They filled me with rich food, political gossip, raucous humor, deep insights, and committed friendships that helped anchor me in my Dallas life.

All of this activity was so fascinating that I was lured away from my little nature preserve and began to show up at political gatherings and meetings, eager to help. I felt a new surge of political hope for change in Texas. But there was also a profound difference for me in this new political world, which was initially a bit disconcerting. I had not been part of Dallas's significant political changes. My hiatus in the nonpartisan world of public television had kept me out of politics for over six years. People and events had moved beyond me. In fact, I was somewhat extraneous—no longer a key player. The big surprise was that it was actually liberating to have opinions without being in charge of anything. I had already consciously chosen a nonpolitical path for my future. I no longer wanted to "run" a campaign or become involved in the daily grind to find and win votes. But I still cared deeply about what was happening. I was just morphing into an observer—not a participant—and becoming surprisingly comfortable in that role. It was gratifying to see fresh new faces—younger people with energy and ideas who were figuring out what they needed to do. Sometimes one of the new operatives might want to "pick my brain" about some new development. Of course that was flattering. But by staying out of the

I continued to make speeches and attend political events even as I retired from active political involvement. Here I'm speaking to a meeting of the Texas AFL-CIO. (Photo courtesy of Alan Pogue)

daily fray, I discovered that I could take a longer, more historical view of what was happening in Texas. I was becoming more analytical and less emotionally involved in the periodic political ups and downs of the Democratic Party.

My longer-term view made me believe that we might be on the cusp of change statewide based on what I was seeing in Dallas. If the conservative Republican old guard was falling apart in Dallas, there were probably also some big cracks in the Republican Party's statewide foundation. When the 2014 gubernatorial election came around, I felt myself being caught up in the muddy well of Texas politics once again—not as a participant but as an increasingly skeptical observer.

A New Book

I followed every detail of what initially appeared to be a hopeful venture when Democrat Wendy Davis ran for governor. She was smart and charismatic, and on some level I thought she might be able to capture the old Ann Richards magic. But her campaign quickly sank. She suffered a devastating loss to the state's lackluster right-wing attorney general, Greg Abbott. I decided to write about what I was seeing and to figure out what went wrong.

I interviewed dozens of partisans—both Republicans and Democrats. I admit that I was more upset with my fellow Democrats than with the Republicans who dashed the party's perennial hope for a new statewide Democratic wave—one more time. To my dismay, the consultants, Democratic Party officials, and even donors seemed to be playing the same old statewide losing game with the same old disastrous results. They appeared to be as delusional about what was really happening on the ground in terms of demographic and cultural shifts as I had been years earlier. In every corner of the state, I began to discover missed opportunities for even moderate success. The failures were massive, and complaints about the Davis campaign's structure, misleading polls, out-of-state consultants, and questionable expenditures were overwhelming. These conversations with local political operatives led me to look more deeply into local and statewide emerging data and trends. I thought I could detect a different pathway that might help Democrats win a few major races in the next election cycle and perhaps even begin to dislodge a few Republican officeholders from their twenty-year tight-fisted grip on every single lever of power in the state.

Of course, I was not alone in seeing these demographic trends. They were becoming more obvious to astute political observers—both Democrats and Republicans. But as far as I knew at the time, no one had put together a public strategy to take advantage of the opportunities that might provide an opening for Democrats. So I guess my ego kicked in, fed by my years of experience on the hustings. I plunged into full-time writing for the first time in years. *Turning Texas Blue: What It Will Take to Break the GOP Grip on America's Reddest State* was published in 2016.[3]

I wrote the book as if I were writing a memo to my fellow Democrats about how they might capture the political future by better understanding the demographic trends and new realities that Texas was now experiencing. It wasn't a surprise that my analysis drew a bit of anger among some of the consultants who benefited from the status quo, but grassroots Democrats across the state took it to heart. When the 2018 election cycle rolled around, a number of candidates who ran for local and statewide office picked up the book to see if they could avoid the same old political traps that had kept Democrats in the pits for twenty years. And some of them did. The changing demographics helped enormously.

Democrats in Houston were able to upend the city's Republican establishment just as Dallas had done a few years earlier. Democratic vote totals also increased dramatically in former solid Republican suburbs. Democrats carried every one of the state's six major cities, picking up several Republican congressional and state legislative seats. And former El Paso congressman Beto O'Rourke came within 2.6 percentage points of defeating Texas senator Ted Cruz. Party alignment was shifting, but 2018 was not yet the year for a major statewide overhaul. Nor was 2020, when Trump swept the presidential election with 52 percent of the statewide vote and Democrats could not pick up a single new seat in the Texas legislature, solidifying their minority status and powerlessness to block extreme right-wing laws and major policy changes.

As disappointed as I was that Democrats could not build on their earlier gains, the 2020 elections actually helped me dispel one of my persistent political illusions and come to terms with the fact that trends cannot predict the outcome of elections. They only provide possibility and hope. Even when demographic trends favor our causes and values, we too often have to overcome legal and cultural barriers as well as the hubris and short-sighted thinking of our own allies. To win, we have to field smart candidates who are less driven by ego and more realistically guided by clear thinking. They, and their donors and followers, have to understand the reality of boundary conditions that encircle their hopes and dreams. They have to adopt pragmatic strategies, raise lots of money, take calculated risks, and undertake serious, hard work to overcome almost insurmountable odds. Texas is still Texas, after all.

Although I was frustrated and dismayed by the turn of events and the increasing fanaticism of so many Texas officials, my desire to finally move away from the exciting political world that had dominated my life seemed more resolute this time. My life on the political hustings, as a player on any level—public or private—finally seemed to be over. Other needs called to me.

Rapt Solitude

I had begun to cope with the enormous changes and isolation brought about by the pandemic in 2020 to read more deeply in science, history, and the novels that I had never taken the time to peruse before. I was especially drawn to biographies and memoirs of women of my generation and older, particularly those who had been writers, artists, or political activists. I wanted to know what their lives had been like and particularly how they had coped with the vagaries of old age, which I had slipped into almost without noticing. And I was starting to write again every day, putting together some of the words that ultimately filled this book.

Even though I didn't really follow her when we were both much younger, I became enthralled by the wisdom of the incomparable poet and musician Patti Smith. In her own advancing years, she articulated the reasons she continued to write. She gave me new words to explain my own growing need to explore my memories for clues I might have missed along the way.

"Why is one compelled to write?" she asks. Her answer is simple: "To channel the future, to revisit childhood, and to rein in the follies and horrors of the imagination for a pulsating race of readers." For Smith it was necessary to "set oneself apart, cocooned, rapt in solitude, despite the wants of others . . . seeking an emptiness to imbue with words." We must write, she says, "engaging in a myriad of struggles, as if breaking in a willful foal. We must write, but not without consistent effort and a measure of sacrifice."⁴

At this time of my life, being "rapt in solitude" has almost become my full-time pursuit; holding on to an "emptiness to imbue with words" is extraordinarily appealing—particularly in the year of the pandemic. Putting words together is still the only way I can really think about anything or force myself to remember what actually happened instead of the illusionary memories I have stored away. It took a lot to get to this point. As wise Florida Scott-Maxwell wrote when she was in her eighties, "You need only claim the events of your life to make yourself yours. When you truly possess all you have been and done . . . you are fierce with reality."⁵

After we reach a certain age, many of us—including myself—become "fierce with reality." And that includes coming to terms with our aches, pains, and physical limitations. We recognize that our circles of influence grow smaller. Our relevancy diminishes. Earlier labels no longer fit us, and newer ones seem simplistic and confusing. There comes a time when none of them matter. My old compulsions seem to have faded away and many of my remaining illusions with them. Now I am simply who I am.

For me, it has been important to learn that coming to terms with fierce reality means that very few complex issues in life—political or personal—are ever completely solved. "Solving" has always been one more of my numerous illusions. I always believed that if I could just figure out exactly what the real problem might be, I could figure out a way to solve it. Now I know that is not always true. Perhaps I am simply more content to let those puzzlements rest for a while and settle for "moments of spontaneous brightness, when the mind appears emancipated," as Patti Smith says. But she also warns those moments are "mere epiphany."⁶ Still, we seek them and appreciate them when they come.

So what am I going to do now?

Whatcha Gonna Do?

Now that I have dipped into my memories in the deep well of Texas politics and emerged fairly intact, I am drawn to something that may have come naturally for my father.

When he was a bit puzzled or blocked by some problem beyond his capacity to solve, my dad would lift his eyebrows, roll his eyes, and utter a typical Sicilian phrase of good-natured acceptance with a shrug of his shoulders: "Whatcha gonna do?" Then he would simply move ahead into the light of life before the shadow of his immediate dilemma could overtake him.[1]

As I have come full circle in my thread of reflections and come to terms with truths I found along the way, I want to keep walking forward into that miraculous light of life that beckoned and sustained my father.

FRANK BERNARD CONIGLIO HAD AN instinct and temperament that allowed him to accept whatever came his way. Some enormous cache of endorphins must have flooded his system when troubles came along, because they seemed to just roll off his back with one of those good-natured shrugs. He had polio as a young man, which left him with recurring physical problems throughout his life. He had wanted to be an architect but spent his young adult life working in his immigrant father's liquor store in downtown Dallas. By the 1950s, however, he was able to use his design talents to become a small-time home builder. Still later, he and my mother owned and ran F. Bernardo's, a small women's fashion boutique in Dallas's original Old Town Center.

While we had a comfortable upbringing, money was always tight. He and my mother lived very simply in their retirement years, carefully measuring expenditures against limited income. No matter what was going on in my dad's outer world, though, he always managed to be the font of pure love for his children, providing the very foundation for our lives. As the father of four girls and a late in life son—my brother, Frank Jr., who is only a year older than my own son, Billy—my dad would have told anyone that he had it all. He was a sponge of sentiment, easily moved to tears by family experiences of sorrow or even joy.

My father had a simple religious faith that sustained him through his own suffering at the end of life. When he was in hospice care and only a few weeks away from death at the age of eighty-six, I asked him if he was afraid. He simply shook his head and quietly said, "No." He told me that he was not worried because he believed that once on the "other side" he would be reunited with his mama and papa and even with my husband, John. Of course, I teased him and told him that I hoped John would be there and not somewhere else, but he was serious. His concept of heaven seemed to provide a source of sublime comfort for him. But he also had an inner reservoir of love and some mysterious deeper peace that emerged as he drifted into old age and sickness. As much as I identified with my amazing mother, I know now that my father may have more to teach me about acceptance of what we cannot avoid. I want to have his peace and serenity to carry to the end of my own life, as he did in those final days of his. I don't know if it will be easy to do so, and maybe it wasn't even easy for him. But he tried. So will I. So what am I gonna do?

Politics was obviously a driving force in my life, along with a compulsive urge to be a player in some larger world of my imagination. And I wanted to write about what I saw and learned. Of course, I also had a desire to do "good," whatever that seemed to be at the moment. And maybe I did the best I could at the time, given my illusions and delusions as well as the circumstances that formed the boundary conditions of my life—location, upbringing, ability, history, relationships, and opportunity. Still, at this time of my life, I feel that there is more. Maybe I just want to live like my father, to be wrapped more fully in peace and serenity each day in order to access those rare moments of pure awareness without striving that he seemed to have. To do so, I will finally have to accept that life is always full of complications, losses, intrigues, doubts, ambiguity, surprises, impulses, fatalism, shadowy fears, and personal inadequacies. But it is also refreshingly tempered with beauty, hope, compelling love, simple pleasures, and the aware-ness that something else is always awaiting us around the corner. So I will keep looking around that corner to find whatever it was that sustained and comforted my father. I might actually have gotten an accidental glimpse of that kind of peaceful acceptance of fate in the midst of a near catastrophe that brought me close to death.

Accidents Happen

Several years ago, I was involved in a serious automobile accident on Interstate 35 just south of Dallas when my sister Martha and I were returning to Austin after a birthday celebration for our father. Mar-tha was driving. We had been on the highway less than an hour when we both were startled by an unusual movement in front of us at what seemed like an extraordinary distance away. Then, very quickly, we real-ized that a car was speeding toward us across the grassy median, which served as a rocket-like projectile for the car because of its incline. Now the car was traveling in the air and beginning to descend directly on top of us. Our hands reached out to hold on to each other as we saw the dark underside of the car just above us. At that moment, I remem-ber clearly thinking: "This is it." I was extraordinarily calm in what seemed like a suspended space of nothingness. Then came the shock as the oncoming car landed on top of us—not directly on the roof of the car, which would have crushed us, but on the trunk. It bounced off our car and continued on its spiraling roll almost a hundred yards behind us, killing its driver and blocking traffic on Interstate 35 for more than two hours. Although covered with glass and small cuts all over our bodies, we had not taken a direct hit. We were miraculously alive.[2]

In the hours and days after the accident, something strange seemed to be happening to me. It was an unfamiliar sense of extraordinary calm, even a feeling of invincibility as if the next impending disaster would not matter because this one did not kill as it should have. I had no anxiety and felt an acceptance of everything around me. I think my sense of peace arose from that split second of knowing that whatever was happening was totally beyond my control. On some deep uncon-scious level, I had calmly accepted my fate.

I later learned that the noted biologist Lewis Thomas believed that at the moment of death the body produces a sufficient amount of endorphins to destroy pain or anxiety.[3] Thomas said that he had seen only one patient die in agony in his whole career, and he attributed that fact to the patient's rabies, which must have destroyed the part of the brain that produces endorphins. For me, in that split second of total "acceptance" of my fate, protective endorphins must have flooded my brain, erasing panic and fear. Of course, the feeling didn't last long. My old anxieties and compulsive behaviors soon reappeared. But the experience was strong enough to lodge in my memory as something valuable, maybe some sort of reassurance about life—and death.

As my life has slowed down, I have continued to ponder that remarkable experience on the road. I now believe that it came close to what Thomas Merton has described as the point of nothingness at the center of our being that is untouched by illusion, creating a moment of pure truth.[4] In that moment I now believe that I had neither illusion nor fear. I think I was just resting within the deeper point of "being."

Since that time, I have been lucky enough to sometimes recapture that "point of nothingness" where illusion and anxiety simply fade away. It has allowed me to understand that within some deeper level of extreme experience I can exist without certainty or predictability. Politics should have taught me the reality of unpredictability, but this is different and deeper within. It is a complete surrender to something ineffable.

Protestant theologian Marcus Borg has used the ancient Celtic con-cept of "thin spaces" to explain these moments of pure acceptance, a form of eloquent calm. Borg has written that reality has at least two layers or dimensions: the visible world of our ordinary experiences and another layer that opens us to moments of sacred calm. When the boundaries between these two levels become very soft, porous, and permeable, something unique happens to us. A veil momentarily lifts, and we have an experience that allows us to rest within a pure state of being without striving.[5] This experience has nothing to do with euphoria or some sort of drug-induced state of ecstasy, and it is not particularly happy. It is more like "nothingness," a subtle "crossing-over" into another dimension contained within our consciousness. It is the feeling that we have access to a deeper sense of awareness that is different from what we ordinarily feel about our life. It is a way of "knowing" within that cloud of "unknowing" that mystics describe. For some of us, it represents the "more" that is possible in our lives. Borg claims that this "more" we experience can actually be called God. Or maybe the feeling simply comes from changes in our brain chemistry. Whatever it is, this mystery of consciousness may be the one feeling in life that makes mere words seem inadequate.

And then what happens? Do we feel infused with divine peace? Or do we simply become aware of an elusive "other" dimension that allows us to rest within it when it comes?

Novelist and essayist Marilynne Robinson believes that this other dimension is actually a different order of reality that places us within the "limbo of the unarticulated and the unacknowledged." It is what she calls grace or the lifting and easing of a burdensome weight.[6] In that other dimension, there is no striving or fear. In a strange way, it does feel weightless.

All I know for certain is that I have sometimes touched that other dimension, or it has touched me. And I have been grateful for that touch, which I now realize is essential to understanding how to acquire the peace that seemed to envelop my father so naturally. Maybe I waited too long to grasp the respite that thin spaces could have offered when I was so deeply engrossed in my passing political show. Or maybe it simply took what it took to recognize another kind of reality when I confronted it head-on.

I can never predict when this deep stillness and absolute acceptance will descend on me. It can never really be anticipated. It just seems to happen, as it did on another day in another unexpected place far away from home.

It was winter. I was walking along a beach on the Pacific coast. A wave rolled across my bare feet and sent a chill through my body. I hunkered down, zipped my jacket, and began to step away from the next cold ripple from the sea. And then something stopped me; some internal signal halted my retreat from the waves. A purposeless peace seemed to wash over me as the next cold wave arrived. I somehow felt once again that "this was it." I could accept whatever comes—the chilling wave, an existence without striving, an end to a political life and the beginning of the shape-shifting nature of my old age. Some form of mysterious acceptance seemed to take hold. I no longer wanted to run away from the encroaching waters or from the challenges of growing old or from those buried memories that revealed the realities, rather than the illusions, of my life.

It is the water again that teaches me. But these rushing waves are not confined or reflected in some deep well of my imagination. They are part of a vast ocean that is larger, deeper, and far grander.

I don't know what the next ripples from the wide sea will bring. But I have patience. I have hope. And so I wait. What will the next wave bring?

Acknowledgments

I AM GRATEFUL TO MY family and friends who exhibited enormous patience with me as I ploughed through old memories to complete this review of personal and political stories that have shaped my journey to self-discovery.

In particular, I want to thank my son, Billy Rogers, and my daughter, Eleanor Rogers Petterson, for their support while I reviewed so many personal aspects of our family life with their father, John Rogers. My sisters, Martha Coniglio and Susie Calmes, and my brother, Frank Coniglio, generously read early versions of this manuscript to make sure that our family memories were in sync.

Several readers of my early efforts, which bear little resemblance to what actually remains in the book, helped me focus on what was most important and to clarify my purpose in writing. I am grateful for the expertise and insight I received from Paul Stekler, Steve Davis, Judy Myers, and Betty Sue Flowers. Other friends read later drafts of the book and encouraged me to continue on this journey, including Fran Vick, Ellen Temple, Bill Cryer, Russell Langley, Jack Martin, and Patsy Martin. I am particularly grateful to my dear friend Mary Mapes, who helped me come up with a book title that clarified what I was trying to say in a simple, direct way. Special thanks for the use of some of his photographs go to the great photojournalist Alan Pogue, whose work has documented the era of Texas politics in which I was most active. I am grateful to my long-time friend Dr. Phyllis Bridges at Texas Woman's University and Kimberly Johnson, director of Special Collections at TWU, who helped us locate the photo of Lady Bird Johnson that we were able to use. Margaret Keys, who has a remarkable institutional memory of life in "old" Austin before the great tech boom and rapid growth of this era, helped me recall the source for one of the other photographs.

Finally, I am grateful to University of Texas Press Director Robert Devens and Editor-in-Chief Dawn Durante, who made the key decision to publish this book. Dawn's support and suggestions enriched and improved the manuscript as we moved along. Freelance copy editor Kathy Lewis was meticulous in her review and UT Press's Robert Kimzey and Joel Pickney stood ready to answer all my questions and keep me on schedule. Historian Dr. Nancy Baker Jones and award-winning novelist Sarah Bird previewed the manuscript for UT Press. Their confidence in the book's value and release was an important milestone for me. My deepest thanks goes to all of the amazing and talented people I've been able to work with over the years, who are far too numerous to mention but who enriched my life beyond measure.

Notes

Introduction

1. Adam Gopnik, *A Thousand Small Sanities: The Moral Adventure of Liberalism* (New York: Basic Books, 2019), 19.

2. Texas was one of the thirty states that quickly ratified the ERA by 1973. And even earlier Texas had passed a state equal rights amendment to the state constitution in 1972. However, a national right-wing backlash against the ERA prevented the measure from securing the support of the thirty-eight states needed for ratification.

3. My adult children, William Douglas (Billy) Rogers and Eleanor Lee Rogers Petterson, have full and interesting lives of their own. I omit most of the intimacies of my life with them to spare them embarrassment. As I age, I am grateful for their closeness, loving companionship, and continuing presence in my daily life.

4. Antonio Damasio, "An End to Suffering" (review of Robert Wright's *Why Buddhism Is True*), *New York Times Book Review*, August 13, 2017.

5. Eudora Welty, *One Writer's Beginnings*, quoted by Maria Popova, Brain Pickings, February 25, 2018 (https://www.themarginalian.org/2018/02/21/eudora-welty-one-writers-beginnings).

6. Alex Williams, "Pete Hamill 'Ain't Done Yet,' He Says," *New York Times*, Sunday, December 1, 2019.

Chapter 1: "Look, There's the Girl"

1. The Foundation for Women's Resources, now called Leadership Women, was chartered as a 501(c)3 nonprofit organization in 1977 by Sarah Weddington, Jane Hickie, Martha Smiley, Ann Richards, and Judith Guthrie.

2. Ruthe Lewin Winegarten (1929–2004) became the foremost advocate of Texas women's history in the state. She was the author or coauthor of over twenty works on women in Texas. She had become a social activist as a teenager, fighting segregation and supporting social services and social justice. At one time, she was the Southwest regional director for the Anti-Defamation League of B'nai B'rith. She was the heart and soul of the Texas Women's History Project.

3. See the exhibition catalogue, *Texas Women: A Celebration of History*, by Mary Beth Rogers, Ruthe Winegarten, and Sherry Smith (Austin: Texas Foundation for Women's Resources, 1981), now in the Special Collections archives at Texas Woman's University in Denton.

4. For a more comprehensive analysis of the Texas Women's History Project and its spinoff efforts, see historian Nancy Baker Jones, "Making Texas Our Texas: The Emergence of Texas Women's History, 1976–1990," *Southwestern Historical Quarterly* 120, no. 3 (January 2017): 278–313.

Chapter 2: A New Texas?

1. After I left the governor's office, Paul Williams became chief of staff for a brief period before Governor Richards appointed him to the State Board of Insurance. Former Texas secretary of state John Fainter, who was a much-respected capital insider, served as chief of staff for the final years of the Richards administration.

Chapter 3: Reality

1. Gopnik, *A Thousand Small Sanities*, 85.

2. William Horton was a convicted felon serving a life sentence for murder in Massachusetts, which instituted a weekend furlough program for prisoners before Dukakis was governor. Horton was released one weekend and failed to return. He committed assault, armed robbery, and rape before being captured and returned to prison. In the 1988 presidential campaign against Governor Dukakis, George H. W. Bush's campaign consultant Lee Atwater created a Willie Horton ad that was clearly racist in tone. It essentially blamed Dukakis for Horton's crimes, although the governor had nothing to do with the prison release program. Similar inflammatory and false attacks in political campaigns are often compared to the Willie Horton ad.

3. *Ruiz v. Estelle*, 550 F.2d 238, was filed by David Ruiz against the Texas Department of Corrections in 1972, claiming that dangerous conditions and procedures within the state's prison system constituted cruel and unusual punishment in violation of the US Constitution. Judge William Wayne Justice ruled in favor of the plaintiffs in 1979 and placed the Texas Department of Corrections under federal oversight of the system. It was not lifted until the state's massive prison building system got underway under Governor Ann Richards in 1994. Federal oversight was not totally withdrawn until 2003.

4. Andrew Cuomo, Mario Cuomo's son, later served as governor of New York until he resigned in 2021 after allegations of sexual harassment were investigated and revealed by the state's attorney general.

5. Edwin "Bud" Shrake (1931–2009) is buried next to Governor Ann Richards in the Texas State Cemetery in Austin. His voluminous papers are housed in the Wittliff Collections at Texas State University in San Marcos.

Chapter 4: Sicily

1. The term "Mezzogiorno" refers to the southern Italian regions, including Sicily, which was once part of the Kingdom of Naples. Its original meaning (Midday) refers to the intensity and position of sunshine at noon in the southern part of the Italian peninsula.

2. Leonardo Sciascscia, as quoted in John Keahey, *Seeking Sicily: A Cultural Journey through Myth and Reality in the Heart of the Mediterranean* (New York: Thomas Dunne Books/St. Martin's Press, 2011), 100.

3. Also with us on the trip were Susie's late husband (Jack Calmes), her daughter and son-in-law (Audrey and Peter Dellgren), and her grandchildren (Ally and Johan Dellgren).

4. The symbol for Sicily is the *Trinacria*, which is on the flag of this autonomous region of Italy. Its origin is mainly mythological, with the head of Medusa at the center surrounded by three legs, which are said to represent three nymphs who danced all around the world, gathering the best fruit, stones, and soil, then threw them into the

sea to create the island of Sicily. This is why, as the saying goes, the island has three corners. The symbol is the certified logo of Sicily, often worked into ceramics and printed materials and placed on buildings. It is also widely sold as a souvenir trinket.

5. Peter Robb, *Midnight in Sicily* (New York: Farrar, Straus & Giroux, 1996).

Chapter 5: The Hard Box

1. Siddhartha Mukherjee, *The Emperor of All Maladies: A Biography of Cancer* (New York: Schriner, 2010). This groundbreaking book explores the broad sweep of this terrible disease and helped me understand on a deeper level the random nature of its excesses as well as the context for so much that had happened in our family over the years.

2. Frank J. Thompson, *Health Policy and the Bureaucracy* (Cambridge, MA: MIT Press, 1981).

Chapter 6: Mr. and Mrs. Extremo

1. Virgil Edward "Red" Berry (1899–1969) represented San Antonio in both the Texas House of Representatives and the Texas Senate in the 1960s. He was widely known for his involvement in gambling in the 1930s–1950s. Pari-mutuel betting and horse racing were finally legalized in Texas in 1987.

2. In addition to Cronkite and Moyers, Lady Bird Johnson, Bill Wittliff, Karen Elliott House, Admiral William McRaven, and more than two dozen Pulitzer Prize winners came through the University of Texas's Journalism School.

3. Willie Morris (1934–1999) became a Rhodes scholar after graduating from the University of Texas. He came back to Texas to become editor of the *Texas Observer* and later the editor-in-chief of *Harper's Magazine*. He then returned to his native Mississippi, where he became writer in residence at the University of Mississippi.

4. The American Newspaper Guild was founded during the Great Depression in the 1930s to represent reporters and writers who were fighting for higher wages and decent working conditions within the newspaper industry. The San Antonio Newspaper Guild Local 25 represented the editorial employees at the *San Antonio Light*, the city's afternoon paper that was part of the national Hearst chain. The American Newspaper Guild changed its name to the News Guild in 2015, reflecting the changing nature and technology of news gathering and reporting.

5. For more information about Albert Peña's life and work, see José Angel Gutiérrez, *Albert A. Peña Jr.: Dean of Chicano Politics* (East Lansing: Michigan State University Press, 2017).

6. For the most comprehensive review of the Democratic Coalition in San Antonio and across Texas, see Max Krochmal, *Blue Texas: The Making of a Multiracial Democratic Coalition in the Civil Rights Era* (Chapel Hill: University of North Carolina Press, 2016).

7. Attorney David Richards's autobiography is the best insider read about how the poll tax was ultimately outlawed in 1966: *Once upon a Time in Texas: A Liberal in the Lone Star State* (Austin: University of Texas Press, 2002).

Chapter 7: Austin

1. In the aftermath of the 2015 mass shooting of African Americans at the historic Mother Emanuel Church in Charleston, South Carolina, and the resulting removal of

dozens of Confederate statues across the country, the name of Robert E. Lee Elementary School in Austin was changed to Russell Lee Elementary. Russell Lee was a famous Works Progress Administration photographer who settled in Austin and taught photography at the University of Texas. My own Stonewall Jackson Elementary School in Dallas became Mockingbird Elementary in 2018.

2. Gerald Sewell and Mary Beth Rogers, with illustrations by Charles Shaw, *The Story of Texas Public Lands: A Unique Heritage* (Austin: Texas General Land Office and the J. M. West Texas Corporation, 1972).

3. Thomas Merton, *New Seeds of Contemplation* (New York: New Directions Paperbook, 1961), 34.

4. Thomas Merton, quoted by Parker Palmer, *On the Brink of Everything: Grace, Gravity & Getting Old* (Oakland, CA: Berrett-Koehler Publishers, 2018), 34.

Chapter 8: Campaigns

1. William Safire, *Safire's Political Dictionary: An Enlarged, Up-to-Date Edition of "The New Language of Politics"* (New York: Random House, 1978), 92.

2. Bart Barnes, "Matt Reese, Veteran Political Consultant, Dies at 71," *Washington Post*, December 3, 1998 (https://www.washingtonpost.com/wp-srv/politics/campaigns/junkie/links/reese.htm).

3. We later learned that having an African American woman as a member of the governing body at Texas A&M generated a storm of complaints among students and donors, which mirrored resentment among conservatives across the state about the administration's numerous appointments of people of color to high decision-making positions.

4. The National Women's Conference was an outgrowth of the United Nations declaration to celebrate International Women's Year in 1975. The conference was created by an executive order of President Gerald Ford to promote equality between men and women. Individual state conferences were held in 1976 to select delegates and determine issues to be covered. I participated in the Texas conference, and Ann Richards was elected to lead the Texas delegation.

5. Jack Martin became a successful international business leader after he left politics. His first company, Public Strategies, served corporate giants like Lockheed Martin, Southwest Airlines, AT&T, and dozens of other major firms. He also was a major consultant to numerous US senators. Later he became head of Hill & Knowlton, one of the nation's largest and most effective global public relations companies, from which he retired as chairman and CEO in 2019.

6. Carole Keeton McClellan (her name at the time) was the first woman elected mayor of Austin. Although she was a Democrat while she served as the three-term mayor, she later became a Republican and was elected to statewide office as comptroller. She lost her challenge to Republican governor Rick Perry in the 2006 general election when she ran as an independent candidate.

7. After he was elected lieutenant governor in 1990, Bob Bullock turned against most of the members of the original Gang of Four. The lieutenant governor has more power over policy than the governor in Texas because of control over legislation. Bullock was notoriously protective of his power, even with his old friend Ann Richards. Later Bullock supported her successor, George W. Bush, and guided Bush's legislative program to success.

8. After John's death in 1987, Sam Kinch and George Phenix carried on with *Texas Weekly* for a while and later sold the publication to another journalist, Ross Ramsey. In 2009 the publication was incorporated into the new digital public interest news site *Texas Tribune*, which Ramsey cofounded with former *Texas Monthly* editor Evan Smith and venture capitalist John Thornton.

9. Dave McNeely, "Political Pro John Rogers Put Passion in Fight for Underdog," *Austin American Statesman*, November 12, 1987.

10. McNeely, "Political Pro John Rogers."

Chapter 9: Women

1. With the major reforms undertaken by the national Democratic Party after losing the 1972 presidential election, the party expanded the number of national committee members to include representatives from various constituency groups. Today national Democrats have an unwieldy party committee structure that can include up to 200 members.

2. Margaret Chase Smith began her career as an elected official when she won a special congressional election to fill the vacancy caused by the death of her husband, Clyde Smith. She served in the US House for almost ten years before being elected to the US Senate in 1949. After serving twenty-four years, she retired in 1973. At the time she was the only woman who had served in both the US House and Senate.

3. Nadine Eckhardt, *Duchess of Palms: A Memoir* (Austin: University of Texas Press, 2009).

4. Celia Morris, *Storming the Statehouse: Running for Governor with Ann Richards and Dianne Feinstein* (New York: Scribner, 1992).

5. For the story of the way African American women were not allowed to vote in the white primary elections held by the state Democratic Party, see Judith N. McArthur and Harold L. Smith, *Minnie Fisher Cunningham: A Suffragist's Life in Politics* (Oxford: Oxford University Press, 2003).

6. Mary Beth Rogers, Ruthe Winegarten, and Sherry Smith, *Texas Women: A Celebration of History*, exhibition catalogue (Austin: Texas Foundation for Women's Resources, 1981), 30, now in the Special Collections archives at Texas Woman's University in Denton.

7. Dr. Gerda Lerner (1920–2013) was one of the founders of the academic field of women's history and became the first female president of the Organization of American Historians. Her writings influenced the approach we took in organizing our research and final exhibition. Eleanor Flexner (1908–1995) wrote the first authoritative narrative about the struggle for women's rights: *Century of Struggle: The Women's Rights Movement in the United States* (Cambridge, MA: Belknap Press of Harvard University Press, 1959).

8. Jovita Idar (1885–1946) was an organizer, writer, and advocate of Mexican American women's rights. She founded La Liga Femenil Mexicanista to provide free instruction for poor Mexican children. She wrote for the Spanish-language newspapers *La Crónica* and *El Progresso*. Christia Adair (1893–1989) was an African American suffragist and later a civil rights leader. Under her leadership of the Houston National Association for the Advancement of Colored People from 1949 to 1959, the chapter grew to 9,000 members, making it one of the largest in the nation.

9. The title "La Pasionaria de Texas" was first bestowed on Tenauyca in a February

28, 1938, *Time Magazine* article about the pecan shellers' strike in San Antonio. It could be loosely translated as "the passionate one."

10. Emma Tenayuca, personal letter to Mary Beth Rogers, July 27, 1981.

11. For a complete list of donors to the Texas Women's History project, see Rogers, Winegarten, and Smith, *Texas Women: A Celebration of History*.

12. Jones is the founding president of the Ruthe Winegarten Foundation for Texas Women's History and was director of research for the *Handbook of Texas* revision project, overseeing the addition of women of color. The project became the digital *Handbook*, which is available online today (https://www.tshaonline.org/handbook). Jessica Brannon-Wranosky served as director of the entire project.

Chapter 10: Roots

1. The 1957 Dallas tornado cut a 20-mile path through West Dallas over about forty minutes and took the lives of ten people, including three children. The sky was clearing as most of the rain had stopped, allowing more than 100,000 people, including me, to watch the tornado rip across the city. As a result, it was the best-documented tornado in history up to that time.

2. Patrick Cox, *Ralph W. Yarborough: The People's Senator* (Austin: University of Texas Press, 2001), 156.

3. For details about the scandal, see Sam Kinch Jr. and Ben Procter, *Texas under a Cloud: Story of the Texas Stock Fraud Scandal* (Austin: Jenkins Publishing, 1972).

4. The legend of the Dirty Thirty lives in political circles because it represented principled rebellion and the kind of bipartisan reform movement we so rarely see today. Because of the efforts of the Dirty Thirty, the 1971 session of the Texas legislature became one of the most progressive in the state's history. New ethics and financial disclosure laws for public officials provided greater transparency as well as allowing greater access to public records and open public meetings. Texas established a public utility commission to rein in the state's private power companies and a sunset review process that made bureaucratic state agencies justify their existence every few years.

Chapter 11: Politics

1. The American Society of Addiction Medicine classifies addiction as a "primary chronic disease of brain reward, motivation, memory, and related circuitry." Like other chronic diseases, addiction often involves cycles of relapse and remission (American Society of Addiction Medicine, https://asam.org).

2. When George W. Bush became president, he would not allow the Securities and Exchange Commission to release documents related to the investigation. When the Texas Rangers ball club was sold in 1998, Bush made a $13 million profit on his investment.

3. Peter Elking and Patricia Sellers, "Richard Rainwater: Remembering a Billionaire Dealmaker," *Fortune*, September 28, 2015 (http://fortune.com/2015/09/28/richard-rainwater-obituary).

4. Bernard Crick, *In Defense of Politics*, 2nd ed. (Chicago: University of Chicago Press, 1982), 24.

5. The phrase "the world as it is versus the world as it should be" is one of the key principles of community organizing taught within the Industrial Areas Foundation

(IAF). I learned the phrase from Ernesto Cortes and it is widely used among the network of organizations all over the nation that are part of the IAF.

Chapter 12: Poland

1. Claude Lanzmann, *Shoah* (documentary, 1985). *Shoah* is a Hebrew word for the mass murder of Jews under the German Nazi regime from 1941 to 1945. It is a biblical term that became the standard word to describe the murder of Jews throughout history.

2. Roger Ebert, *Shoah*, December 29, 2010 (https://www.rogerebert.com/reviews /great-movie-shoah-1985).

3. Jacob Mikanowski, "In Warsaw, the Stones Remember," *New York Times*, Sunday, February 18, 2018.

4. Andrew Higgins, "Poland's Solidarity Movement Is the Opposite of What It Was," *New York Times International*, July 29, 2021.

5. Karlfried Graf Dürckheim (1896–1988) explained his belief in an adversary principle in an interview with Alphonse Goettmann in *Dialogue on the Path of Initiation: An Introduction to the Life and Thought of Karlfried Graf Dürckheim* (New York: Globe Press Books, 1991).

6. Anne Applebaum, *Twilight of Democracy: The Seductive Lure of Authoritarianism* (New York: Doubleday, 2020), 16.

7. "Hope Is a Powerful Weapon," letters from Nelson Mandela, excerpts printed in the *New York Times*, Sunday, July 8, 2018.

8. Reinhold Niebuhr, *The Children of Light and the Children of Darkness* (New York: Charles Scribner's Sons, 1944), 9–13.

9. Quoted by Maria Popova from *Selected Letters of C. G. Jung, 1909–1961*, online newsletter (Brain Pickings), December 12, 2001 (https://www.themarginalian.org/page/2).

Chapter 13: Words

1. Zadie Smith, quoted in Brain Pickings (https://www.themarginalian.org/2020/08 /13/zadie-smith-intimations-something-to-do).

2. Christine Stephens became a top official and mentor to dozens of young community organizers within the Industrial Areas Foundation. She died in 2019. Pearl Ceasar retired from IAF organizing and became superior general of her religious order, the Congregation of Divine Providence.

3. Dr. Betty Sue Flowers headed the prestigious Plan II liberal arts program at the University of Texas and was later the director of the LBJ Presidential Library. After her retirement, she became an international consultant based in New York.

4. Mary Beth Rogers, *Cold Anger: A Story of Faith and Power Politics* (Denton: University of North Texas Press, 1990). After I left active politics and moved to Dallas in 2004, I became a board member of the Interfaith Education Fund, the nonprofit education arm of the Southwest Interfaith Network that provided training for local leaders and new organizers. In 2016 I joined the nonpartisan board of the national Industrial Areas Foundation, the umbrella organization that supports local community organizing efforts all over the nation.

5. John Egerton, *Speak Now Against the Day: The Generation before the Civil Rights Movement in the South* (Chapel Hill: University of North Carolina Press, 1994).

6. Mary Beth Rogers, *Barbara Jordan: An American Hero* (New York: Bantam-Doubleday, 1998).

Chapter 14: Change

1. KLRU's original licensing agreement for the annual *Austin City Limits* Music Festival was with a group of young Austin entrepreneurs who founded C3 Presents. The national firm Live Nation took 51 percent ownership of C3 Presents in 2013 and now runs the festival. *Austin City Limits* has a storied history. Bill Arhos, my predecessor as CEO of KLRU, created the music series in 1974, just as the Austin music scene was becoming central to the cultural life of the city. Terry Lickona joined the station in 1978 and ultimately became the executive producer of the show, which is the longest-running music show on television. Over the years, he also broadened the range of the show to include blues, folk, jazz, rock, and many crossover artists.

2. Annie's List was started in 2003 to recruit, train, support, and elect women to the Texas legislature and other offices. Since then Annie's List has helped more than 100 women win office. In 2017 I did some consulting and planning work with Annie's List when its visionary leader, Patsy Martin, took it to a higher level of operation and effectiveness. The organization bears the name of Annie Webb Blanton, the first woman elected to statewide political office in Texas, in 1918.

3. Mary Beth Rogers, *Turning Texas Blue: What It Will Take to Break the GOP Grip on America's Reddest State* (New York: St. Martin's Press, 2016).

4. Patti Smith, *Devotion* (New Haven: Yale University Press, 2017), 87.

5. Florida Scott-Maxwell, *The Measure of My Days*, quoted by Parker Palmer, *On the Brink of Everything: Grace, Gravity & Getting Old* (Oakland, CA: Berrett-Koehler Publishers, 2018), 173.

6. Patti Smith, *Year of the Monkey* (New York: Alfred A. Knopf, 2019), 95.

Chapter 15: Whatcha Gonna Do?

1. The concept of "walking toward the light" is taken from John 12:35 (Revised Standard Version). Jesus tells his followers, "Walk while you have the light, lest the darkness overtake you; he who walks in the darkness does not know where he goes."

2. The woman who was killed while driving that car was not at fault in the accident. Another car passing at high speed had bumped her vehicle, causing it to swerve out of control into the median and incoming traffic. The speeding driver never stopped.

3. Lewis Thomas, *The Lives of a Cell: Notes of a Biology Watcher* (New York: Bantam Books, 1974).

4. Thomas Merton, *Conjecture of a Guilty Bystander* (New York: Doubleday & Co., 1965), 142, quoted by Father Richard Rohr in his Daily Meditation, Center for Action and Contemplation, Daily Meditation Archives, August 31, 2020 (https://cac.org).

5. Marcus J. Borg, *The Heart of Christianity: Rediscovering a Life of Faith* (New York: HarperOne, 2015), 155–156.

6. Marilynne Robinson, *The Givenness of Things* (New York: Farrar, Straus & Giroux, 2015), 273–275.

Index

Photos are indicated by italicized page numbers.

United Nations Association, 181
University of Texas, 41
University of Texas Law School, 151
unpredictability, in politics, 113

values, core, 165
Velasquez, Willie, 91
Voting Rights Act, 112, 117, 133, 149
vulnerabilities, 8–9, 57; insights on, 18; masking, 14

Walesa, Lech, 172, 174
Walt Disney Company, 162
Watson, Kirk, 195
Weddington, Sarah, 15–16, 21, 22, 133
Welty, Eudora, 6
Werden, Frieda, 135
White, Mark, 25, 123, 124
Whole Foods Market, 111
"widow's succession," 130
Williams, Clayton, 25, 26

Williams, Monte, 25
Williams, Paul, 23–24, 25, 31, 47, 56
Wilson, Eddie, 103
Winegarten, Ruthe, 21, 135, 139, 140, 144
women, 129, 152–153; as dragon ladies, 130–131; little-known, 148–149; organizations of, 136–137; Second Wave Women's Movement, 3, 24, 133–135; Texas Women's History Project, 21, 135, 135–138, 141–144
Women's Army Corps, 143
Women's Hall of Fame, 141
Workers Alliance, 139
workers laws, 134
workshops, campaign, 115–116, 118–119
World War II, 137
Wynne, Anne, 25

Yarborough, Ralph, 84, 102, 123, 145, 147–148, 149, 153
Yeltsin, Boris, 169–170